LUKE

BIBLE STUDY
COMMENTARY

LUKE

BIBLE STUDY COMMENTARY

VIRTUS E. GIDEON

ZONDERVAN
PUBLISHING HOUSE
OF THE ZONDERVAN CORPORATION
GRAND RAPIDS, MICHIGAN 49506

Library of Congress Catalog Card Number 67-22691

Eighth printing 1981
ISBN 0-310-24973-2

Printed in the United States of America

To
My Wife Bobbye,
and
Tim,
Our Son

Preface

This book is not intended to be a complete commentary on the gospel of Luke but is rather intended to serve as a guide in a study of the gospel. The text of Luke should always be read in conjunction with the section headings and discussions. The *Study Guide* proposes to outline the gospel in logical form and then give guidance to the reader as he studies each section. Discussions of grammatical and syntactical relationships are kept to a minimum. The *Study Guide* is prepared with the student and pastor in view.

Special acknowledgments must be recorded. The author is indebted to Zondervan Publishing House, Grand Rapids, Michigan, who requested the manuscript. Their cooperation in the writing and publishing of this manuscript is deeply appreciated. The author is likewise indebted to Miss Jo Ann Greene, a student at Southwestern Baptist Theological Seminary, Fort Worth, Texas, for her assistance in typing the initial drafts. A tremendous indebtedness to Mrs. Harry O. Hickman for typing and editing of the final draft could not be exaggerated. Suggestions of fellow professors also proved helpful.

This study is published with the hope that it will lead the pastor and student to a deeper appreciation for Luke's gospel and thereby make the ministry and teaching of Jesus more meaningful.

—VIRTUS E. GIDEON

Southwestern Baptist Theological Seminary
Fort Worth, Texas

Contents

Part I

Introduction and Background

The gospel of Luke has long been recognized as the gospel which presents Jesus as the Universal Saviour. This gospel, along with Matthew and Mark, is numbered among the synoptics; its primary purpose is to present Jesus as the Saviour of all men, Jew and Gentile alike. Written in some of the best and most idiomatic Greek of the New Testament, its message reaches from the simplest presentation of gospel truth to that which is most sublime. Contained within its structure are some of the best loved parables spoken by Jesus. The parable of the lost sheep, the parable of the lost coin, and the parable of the prodigal son are among those which immediately come to mind. Coupled with such famous parables as these are accounts of the virgin birth, the experience with Zacchaeus, the Sermon on the Plain, the Master's weeping over Jerusalem, the Emmaus record, and the Ascension account.

The Author. The Luke-Acts material has traditionally been accepted as derived from a common source. The author seems to refer to the gospel as "the first treatise" (Acts 1:1), both Acts and Luke are addressed to Theophilus (Luke 1:3; Acts 1:1), and the Greek of the two is almost identical. The author of Acts was obviously a member of Paul's missionary party, at least beginning with the "we" sections in Acts 16:10 ff. Scholars have long agreed that Luke is described by Paul as the beloved physician (Colossians 4:14). The gospel of Luke abounds with medical terminology, and the presence of this language can best be explained by the suggestion that the author was a physician; thus he was intensely interested in the "medical" miracles of our Lord. Luke has traditionally been recognized as a Gentile, (although within recent years some students have suggested that he was Jewish), thus the only Gentile author contributing to the New Testament canon.

The preface of the gospel indicates that the author was a careful historian, first evaluating carefully the sources and not accepting gullibly any or all statements concerning Jesus. In the preface (Luke 1:1-4) the author meticulously states that gospel writing was a popular work in his day and that he has researched the many gospels already written. He proceeds, however, to disclose that this gospel was written in order that Theophilus might know the certainty of the things pertaining to Jesus.

The Nature of the Gospel. The universal Gospel presents Jesus as the Saviour of the world, not merely the Messiah of the Jews. Theophilus was probably a Gentile, and thus the content of Luke's gospel is aimed primarily toward the Gentile world. The gospel is dated in relationship to the current Roman emperor and Roman governors of the Biblical lands, not in relationship to Jewish thought or prophecy. Luke was not interested in presenting the life of Jesus as the fulfillment of Jewish prophecy; therefore, Old Testament materials are infrequently quoted. The habit of translating Hebrew words into their Greek equivalents is further evidence that this gospel is universal in scope. For example, Simon the Canaanite is introduced by Luke as Simon the Zealot. Still additional evidence for the universal nature of the gospel is in the nature of the genealogical record which differs from that of Matthew—the only other gospel containing the genealogical record of our Lord—in that Luke traces the record to Adam, the first man, and not to Abraham, the head of the Jewish race.

The universality of this gospel is further demonstrated in several ways. The kingdom of heaven is open to the Samaritans (Luke 9:51-56); the only grateful leper who returned to thank the Lord for personal healing was a Samaritan (Luke 17:11-19); praise was heaped upon the Roman centurion because of his great faith (Luke 7:9). Even a cursory reading of the gospel provides many other evidences, but these suffice to indicate the universal claim which Jesus lays to man's heart.

The purpose of the gospel is defined in the universality of this nature. As one of the synoptic gospels, this writing joins the group in presenting Jesus' ministry from the same basic viewpoint. The term "synoptic" means a seeing together; thus the synoptic gospels describe Jesus' ministry from the same perspective. Yet, each of these gospels contains materials peculiar to itself, particularly Matthew and Luke. The gospel of Luke is especially unique in its presentation of the

Perean ministry of our Lord, the record itself forming the bulk of the central section of the gospel.

The Date. Mark is generally accepted as the earliest of the synoptic gospels and formed the framework for the other two synoptics. Few verses are peculiar to Mark's gospel. The source critic, a scholar who attempts to define the sources which a writer employed, has demonstrated that perhaps as few as 26 verses are not repeated in Matthew and Luke. It is apparent from the introduction to Acts (1:1 ff.) that this material was written following the gospel of Luke. Acts concludes with the account of Paul's arrival in Rome and his two years' sojourn in his own hired house. History dates Paul's arrival in Rome in approximately A.D. 60; Acts must have been written in approximately A.D. 62. Inasmuch as Luke was written prior to the Acts material, this gospel can logically be dated A.D. 60-61.

The Gospel's Relationship to Other Canonical Gospels. The gospel of Luke presents Jesus as the Universal Saviour, while the gospel of Mark stresses the work of Jesus. Mark apparently wrote to the Romans, who would be interested in the active Lord. Matthew wrote to the Jews, proving that Jesus is the Jewish Messiah. John's gospel, written later and from a perspective unique to himself, has long been recognized as the spiritual gospel. His gospel is described as an evangelistic writing (John 20:31). Each gospel has its own place and message. Our understanding of Jesus would be greatly hampered if Luke's gospel were not included. This thrilling work stresses the universal nature and scope of God's redemptive purpose as exhibited in the ministry of His Son.

CHAPTER ONE

Luke's Introduction to His Gospel

The introduction to his gospel is unique. Although the other gospel writers plunge immediately into their narratives concerning the life of Jesus (or pre-existent state as in John's gospel), Luke sets a background against which to present Jesus as the Universal Saviour. The preface (vss. 1-4) is actually one lengthy sentence. Luke is the only gospel writer to employ the personal pronoun "I" in gospel materials. He immediately identifies himself with the message to be presented, but at the same time draws the curtain to permit his readers an insight into the careful research and construction of his message. The following facts are important to one's comprehension of Luke's ability as a historian and are also important to an interpretation of his message.

The Popularity of Gospel Writing. The occasion for Luke's attempt to construct an account of the life and ministry of his Lord is indicated by the phrase, "For as much as many have taken in hand to set forth in order. . . ." The "many" are left undefined by Luke, but he likely includes personalities other than those connected with canonical materials. Included in Luke's reference would be "gospel" accounts which have not been preserved.

The popularity of gospel writing is indicative of the intense prominence enjoyed by the Saviour. The tremendous impact of Jesus' life and ministry upon the world of His time cannot be minimized. So long as the impact of His ministry was felt basically by the Jewish nation, gospel records were not so essential as they became in the day when the Saviour's redemptive purpose began to touch the Gentile world. The Jews had been trained in memorization, and the many interpretations of the law, both written and oral, were passed from generation to generation by this means. However, with the conversion of Gentiles it became essential to record the life and ministry of

Jesus. These people were not skilled in the art of memorization as were the Jews, neither were they acquainted with the religious facts which the Jews possessed simply because of their religious background. Remember that the eyewitnesses of Jesus' ministry were limited numerically and were too few in number to declare to all the new Christians the historical events surrounding the life of Jesus. This numerical limitation required the collecting of stories concerning Jesus' ministry. These accounts were used for instruction and teaching. Furthermore, as the kingdom grew and the years passed, some of the apostles suffered martyrdom. Link with these factors the fact that all the apostles by this time (A.D. 60) were aged men. Why these accounts were collected and later were enlarged into fuller and more complete records of the Saviour's life and ministry can easily be understood.

The Content of the Writing. The many writers to whom Luke refers in verse one attempted to record "those things which are most surely believed . . ." The words "concerning the deeds which stand fulfilled among us" more accurately translate the K.J.V. expression "most surely believed among us." The participle (stand fulfilled) is derived from a verb which means "to bring to completion" or "to make full." The term means "to bring to a point of completion," or "to overflow."

This content is further defined as having been the testimony of eyewitnesses and "ministers of the word." These are events of certainty, and they occurred "among us." Luke gleaned these materials from eyewitnesses. The term "eyewitness" is a word which means "to see with one's own eyes, self-sight." This is the Greek term from which the medical word "autopsy" is derived. Contemporary Greek medical writers often employed this term. Not only did "self-seers" deliver these traditions to Luke, but "underrowers" (or servants) — one who rows at the command of another—also related their experiences to Luke. The English term "minister" does not signify official clergy, but rather refers to an individual who serves a superior. These were servants of the Word, that is, the gospel message.

His Purpose in Writing. Verse three explains and justifies Luke's purpose in composing a gospel narrative. Others had embarked upon such an adventure with less information than Luke possessed. But Luke writes that Theophilus might know the certainty of those things in which he had been instructed.

The term "know" is a compound verb meaning "full knowledge." Luke then writes that Theophilus might know completely, that he might have knowledge in addition to the information already possessed. Theophilus had been instructed in the words relating to the Saviour, and Luke's message serves to complement the instructions already received by Theophilus.

Numerous suggestions have been offered concerning the identity of Theophilus. Some interpreters believe him to be an individual, the name itself meaning "a lover of God." Others have suggested that the term "Theophilus" does not refer to a person but is merely a symbolic name for all Christians. Still others have suggested that Theophilus is a Roman governmental official, and Luke wrote to placate him. A popular approach has been to suggest that Luke wrote to Theophilus, the governmental official, to secure his assistance in gaining Paul's release from prison.

His Method of Research. Luke indicates in verse three that he traced accurately the course of all things from the very beginning of Jesus' life. The term "accurately" indicates that he went into the minutiae of the events surrounding the life of Jesus. Not only did he check into the most minute details, he also traced all these things from the first. Add to this his purpose to write "in order" and one can readily see his carefulness as a researcher and author. The careful researcher was no gullible historian, but found it essential to satisfy himself concerning the reliability of his materials. Luke investigated recent accounts of the ministry of Jesus and traced these from the very first. The accuracy and integrity of his message have stood the test of endless critical research and countless attempts to destroy the veracity of his gospel.

FOR FURTHER STUDY

1. Read the article entitled "Luke" in *The New Smith's Bible Dictionary,* p. 218.
2. Read the article entitled "The Gospel of Luke" in *The Interpreter's Dictionary of the Bible,* pp. 180-188.
3. Read the article entitled "Apocrypha, N.T." in *The Interpreter's Dictionary of the Bible,* pp. 166-168. Note the differences between Luke and these gospels.
4. Read the "Luke" article in *The Zondervan Pictorial Bible Dictionary,* p. 494 ff.

CHAPTER TWO

Background to the Saviour's Ministry

Luke introduced the Saviour's ministry by painting the backdrop of events relating to the birth of Jesus, then passing through the youth experiences, and ultimately to the initiation of the public ministry. The introduction to Jesus' ministry is characterized by such accounts as the angel's visits prior to the births of John and Jesus, their births, the youth of the Saviour, and subsequently Jesus' detailed personal preparation for His ministry.

1. *Events Preceding the Births of John and Jesus, 1:5-56*. As in the interbiblical literature, so in Luke's gospel, angels are important as messengers of God. But preceding the introduction of the angel's visit to Zacharias, the historian is extremely careful to pinpoint the historical setting. This event occurred when Herod was the king of Judea, and Zacharias, of the priestly group of Abia, was performing his priestly responsibilities in the Temple. As a priest, Zacharias would of necessity have been a descendant of Aaron, and this family relationship automatically qualified him for the priesthood. The priests were too numerous to serve simultaneously in the Temple. Therefore, they had been divided into twenty-four groups, each group alternating in responsibility except during Passover, Pentecost, and the Feast of the Tabernacles. All of the priests served during these feasts, but during the remainder of the year they served only twice and that for a period of one week. Luke's research ability is also indicated by his notation that Zacharias was married to a descendant of Aaron.

(1) *Angelic Ministers, 1:5-38*. The number of priests precluded all being involved in performing the more exciting Temple responsibilities such as the burning of incense. Duties were divided during the six secular days, but all of the course served on the Sabbath, at which time individual services were determined by lots. It had fallen Zacharias' responsibility to burn incense; perhaps this was the only

15

time in his life that he would have this responsibility. This service brought the priest particularly near God. While he burned the incense, the people were outside in prayer.

a. *Prediction of John's Birth, 1:5-25.* An angel stood on the right side of the altar of incense and spoke to Zacharias, who was troubled because of the angel's presence. However, the angel reassured him by saying: "Stop fearing, Zacharias, because your prayer was heard, and your wife Elizabeth will bear a son to you and you will call his name John. And joy and gladness shall be to you and many will rejoice at his birth." Although the term "many" simply refers to a number of people, it is also the term used to refer to the common people (*hoi polloi*). This son was to bring joy not only to an aged father and mother, but also to the multitudes of the world. The angel further indicated that the son was not to be given the name of his father, but was to be called "John." The son was to be a Nazarite (Numbers 6:3) and was to be filled with the Holy Spirit, "even from his mother's womb." The mission of John was described as a mission of preparation in the power of Elijah (1:17). See Malachi 3:1.

Zacharias, the aged and righteous priest, questioned the angel. How can a man so old become a father? How can a wife as aged as Elizabeth become the mother? At this point in the conversation, the angel identified himself as Gabriel, a messenger of God who stands in the immediate presence of the Father. The truth of Gabriel's message was to be verified by Zacharias' inability to speak until these predicted events had occurred. During this extended conversation, the people prayed for the return of Zacharias and the report that the incense had been burned. When the priest returned to the people, he was unable to relate the experience of his spiritual service in their behalf; nor was he able to recount for the worshipers the experience with Gabriel.

After completing his days of service, Zacharias returned to his home and Elizabeth conceived as Gabriel had promised (1:23-25). Her conception prompted her to give all the credit and glory to God for this blessing; she indicated that the Lord had taken away her reproach, which was felt so keenly by any childless Jewish wife. It was only natural that the husband desired an heir, the mother desired a child, and the Jewish people desired a Messiah. Therefore, childlessness was exceedingly difficult for the Jewish wife to accept. Now, Elizabeth knew peace of mind inasmuch as her physical condition had become what Gabriel had promised her husband. During the first five months of her pregnancy, Elizabeth withdrew from public life. Luke does not indicate the purpose of her withdrawal, but it is unlikely that she kept herself from society in order to conceal her pregnancy. More likely Elizabeth withdrew in order to glorify God privately for the fulfillment of His promise. By this time Zacharias would have communicated by some means all the Temple events to his wife, and this sharing would have further strengthened Elizabeth's faith.

b. *Prediction of Jesus' Birth, 1:26-38.* The activity of Gabriel was not limited to the conversation with Zacharias. In the sixth month of Elizabeth's pregnancy, Gabriel appeared to Mary, a virgin, and disclosed the good news that God had chosen her to become the mother of His Son. Luke 1:26-27 again underscores the carefulness with which Luke recorded the events. Every detail seems to be spelled out in simplicity. Nazareth, a Galilean village, was located approximately 70 miles northeast of Jerusalem on the northern edge of the Plain of Esdraelon. Situated in a valley, Nazareth was surrounded by hills on all sides except the southern side. In a simple Galilean village, Gabriel delivered the Father's message to Mary, a virgin unmarried but betrothed to Joseph, a descendant of David. Betrothal was regarded as sacred, and any violation by either party was judged by the Jews to be adultery. The initial greeting indicates that Mary had received favor from the Father, and in this sense she is blessed among all women. However, this does not carry with it the idea that she was able to bestow favor; rather, she had received favor from the Father. Mary was troubled by the angel's report but Gabriel allays her fear in the command, "Stop fearing, Mary!" This is the same expression which he used to minimize the fear of Zacharias. The Greek construction indicates that Mary was already afraid and that Gabriel insisted that she stop fearing; she had found grace with God. He further indicated that she would conceive and bear a son, His name being Jesus. The significance of the name "Jesus" immediately struck a responsive chord within the heart of Mary inasmuch as this is the Greek equivalent of the "Joshua" of the Old Testament. Luke 1:32 defines Jesus as the Son of the Highest, the One who is to rule over the throne of David, and One who will have an unending kingdom (1:33).

Although the announcement must have thrilled the young virgin, she immediately objected to the reality of the experience, basing her objection upon a simple statement of fact—she was unmarried. The tremendous impact of Luke 1:35 is often overshadowed by the simplicity in which it is stated. Gabriel's simple explanation of her conception is that Mary will become pregnant through the divine influence manifested in the working of the Holy Spirit. The Son to be born of Mary would be the Son of God. The angel was explicit in indicating that God would be revealed as a divine being in this experience. Gabriel further declares that this Son to be begotten through Mary will be holy, thus free from all sin. Paul (Galatians 4:4) indicated that the Redeemer was "born of woman." Thus, God identified Himself with man, revealing Himself in human flesh. The statement of His sinlessness cannot be overemphasized, for the Redeemer of man Himself is holy. No sinful being could reconcile man to God.

The New Testament makes no attempt to prove the virgin birth. Luke and Matthew record it; Paul indicates that the Redeemer was born of a woman; but the New Testament as a whole accepts the doctrine of the virgin birth as being harmonious with the life of the Saviour whose miracles and ministry explain the existence of the New Testament. And the explanation of Gabriel was equally simple. He revealed Elizabeth's experience to Mary, her kinswoman, concluding that nothing is impossible with God. Mary's response to the annunciation was in simple, yet sublime words (1:38). This was no trivial matter! Likely every Jewish woman for several hundred years had longed for such a pronouncement from God, but young, unassuming Mary had been chosen to become the mother of God's Son. The honor could not be denied; but the social pressure occasioned by such an experience must have been almost unbearable, not only in the future months but even immediately in the mind of the young betrothed virgin. Did she disclose this conversation to Joseph? The account in Matthew (1:18-25) leads one to believe that she did not discuss the facts with him; the angel's appearance to Joseph resolved whatever problem he had concerning Mary's pregnancy prior to their marriage. Consequently, the words of Mary, "Be it unto me according to thy word," expressed a modest and quiet faith originating in the heart of a young virgin committed to God.

(2) *Mary's Visit to Elizabeth, 1:39-45.* Gabriel (1:36) suggested by implication that Mary should visit Elizabeth. The contextual record indicates that Mary responded quickly to the suggestion of Gabriel. Gabriel (1:36) disclosed that Elizabeth was in the sixth month of her pregnancy; Mary (1:56) spent approximately three months with Elizabeth before returning to her own home. The text further records (1:57) that Elizabeth's son was not born until after Mary had returned to her own home. Some commentators have

suggested that Mary's visit was in conjunction with Joseph's desire to "put her away privately." However, this conjecture finds no actual basis in the historical account, as one can readily see from comparing the verses previously mentioned. Mary visited Elizabeth soon after her confrontation with Gabriel. No one would have known so soon of her pregnancy, not even Joseph. Leaving Nazareth, Mary journeyed to the village located in the hill country in southern Judea, a journey requiring four or five days.

When Mary greeted Elizabeth, her kinswoman (not necessarily cousin), Elizabeth's baby immediately moved. The movement of unborn babies during the sixth month of pregnancy is not unusual, but this particular demonstration was extraordinary inasmuch as Elizabeth realized what had happened to Mary through the working of the Holy Spirit. In this moment of ecstatic excitement she cried, "Blessed are you among women and blessed is the fruit of thy womb." This recognition is further demonstrated in the question of 1:43: "Whence is this to me, that the mother of my Lord should come to me?" Elizabeth, showing no signs of envy or animosity, recognized the honored position enjoyed by Mary and further explained this recognition on the basis of the baby's movement being connected with the word of Mary's greeting. Her humility was clearly revealed in that she defined Mary's visit as an additional honor. Thus, the mother of the one destined to prepare the way for the Messiah joined her unborn child in honoring the person of the one selected by God to become the Saviour's mother.

(3) *Mary's Hymn of Praise, 1:46-56.* That Mary's praise did not begin with the annunciation is noteworthy; rather, her magnificent words of thanksgiving originated with the experience in the household of Zacharias and Elizabeth. It seems as if her extemporaneous reactions were brought about by the actions of Elizabeth's unborn baby and the testimony offered by Elizabeth. This hymn of praise has been traditionally known as the "Magnificat." The Hebrew style of this hymn is readily seen, and scholars have long referred to this as a lyrical poem. The hymn is in sharp contrast to the words so recently offered by Elizabeth, who obviously spoke rather tempestuously and boisterously. Mary's hymn was characterized by humility and holiness. The Magnificat is characterized by Old Testament expressions to which Mary gave deeper meanings. Mary praised God for the present and subsequent honor which He had brought her (1:46-49). She recognized all this to be an evidence of God's eternal mercy (1:54). Mary's concluding statement (1:55) is a recognition

that God is fulfilling His promise to Abraham and his seed. The circumstances surrounding Mary's visit to Elizabeth, the exclamations of Elizabeth, and Mary's hymn of praise are indeed unusual and unique. Never before had the world witnessed such workings! Nor has the world witnessed such events in the days following! Two women of simple life and circumstance were strangely blessed of God—one becoming a mother in old age that her son might be the forerunner of the Messiah, the other chosen to be the mother of the Redeemer.

Man could wish for the ability to draw the curtains of time and to discover the conversations and sharing between Elizabeth and Mary during the three months they were together. They were the only ones in the house who could speak to each other; Zacharias remained dumb. In all probability, they communicated with him in writing, even as he communicated with others by this means at a later time (1:63).

2. *The Birth of John, 1:57-80.* Less than twelve months had passed since the time of Gabriel's appearance to Zacharias. Many interwoven events had occurred during this period, including the angel's visit to Mary, his appearance to Joseph, Mary's visit to Elizabeth, the pregnancies of the two women, the untold hours of meditation upon these miraculous events, and all the excitement which normally accompanies the birth of a child. Mary had remained with Elizabeth for three months, and Elizabeth's child was born soon after Mary's departure. Neighbors and relatives joined this aged couple in their rejoicing and praised God for the manifestation of His mercy upon the barren Elizabeth; He had given her a son.

Many events occurred according to Jewish custom. The birth of a child was automatically a time of rejoicing in the Jewish home, particularly if the child was a boy. The birth of the child had doubtless occasioned rejoicing by the parents and relatives and merrymaking brought by musicians. This excitement had not subsided before time for the circumcision ceremonies which were scheduled the eighth day. This was the day for the naming of the boy; girls were named any time within thirty days of their birth.

The Jews characteristically selected meaningful names. However, under circumstances such as these, one would expect that the child would automatically be named for his father. Yet strangely, even Elizabeth insisted upon the name "John" (1:63). This information she had gathered from Zacharias during the time of his dumbness. Although the numerous relatives "made signs" to Zacharias and insisted that Elizabeth must be mistaken in the selection of the name, the aged priest himself wrote on the tablet the simple words, "His name is John." No one could debate the issue with Zacharias and Elizabeth. The question of the name had already been settled. Gabriel had given the name at the time of his visit to Zacharias.

At that point, Zacharias recovered his speech. He was continually speaking in the manner of praising God. Such events as these could not long remain secret. With the holiday-like atmosphere which surrounded the circumcision and naming of the young boy, there was also an immediate still and calm brought by this experience just witnessed. The steadfast refusal of the parents to name the child for his father, followed by the miraculous loosing of the father's tongue, surely indicated that this was no ordinary naming and circumcision ceremony. Those humble folk returned to their hill country homes realizing the source of this child. The name itself means, "God has graciously given." Even while the people questioned the future responsibilities of this child, the hand of the Lord was with him to support him in the power of God. John was to be strengthened and to be led to his life's work.

During the time of Mary's and Elizabeth's conversations, Zacharias had been silenced. Now his speech had been recovered and his song or prophecy is called the "Benedictus," named for its first word in the Vulgate. This song is divided into two parts, the first being vss. 68-75, and the second composed of vss. 76-79. The first section addresses itself to the salvation which is about to appear in the person of the Messiah, Mary's child, and indicates that God has again visited and redeemed His people. This redemption is defined as a "visit." It is further defined as raising up a "horn of salvation" (1:69), a figure of speech contained in the Old Testament and based upon the strength of the wild bull's horn (Ezekiel 29-21). This salvation was to come through the household of David just as it had been prophesied by the holy prophets. This salvation to be provided through the Messiah was to be constituted by a deliverance from enemies, a fulfillment of the promise of mercy which had been given the ancestors, the remembering of the holy covenant and the oath given to Abraham, and a fearless service to be rendered in holiness and righteousness throughout life.

The second section of the Benedictus relates to the child himself. John was to be called the prophet of the Highest and was to prepare the way for the Lord. This preparation would be constituted by the proclamation of forgiveness, the spreading of spiritual light to those in spiritual darkness, and a guidance into a peaceful way—

all of which would be enjoyed in the tender mercy of God. Dark and unpredictable days were drawing to a conclusion. A new day was dawning. The Messianic Age for which Israel had so long prayed was about to be introduced.

Luke's only reference to the childhood of John is 1:80. This brief verse states that John was continuing to grow and was gaining strength in body and spirit. John lived in the desert hills while the Messiah was to live and work as a carpenter in Nazareth, each waiting until the proper time for his introduction to the world. One could wish that the silence of these years were broken but he must be satisfied with the simple statement concerning the child's physical and spiritual development, his dedication, and his patient waiting until the time that God's eternal purpose should be introduced into the heart of man.

3. *The Birth of Jesus, 2:1-40.* Luke had now established the background for the Saviour's coming. He had told the story of the angel's visits to Mary, Elizabeth, and Joseph, and had disclosed the birth of John. Yet, 1:80 goes beyond the time of Jesus' birth and takes the reader to the subsequent manhood of John, the forerunner of the Saviour.

(1) *The Account of the Birth, 2:1-7.* Luke meticulously established the historical circumstances surrounding the birth of the promised Messiah. He indicated that a decree from Caesar Augustus, who ruled Rome from 30 B.C. until August 19, A.D. 14, demanded the taxation of the entire Roman Empire. The dogma from Caesar involved a census of the entire Roman world; taxation naturally and normally followed and was based upon the census. Luke indicated that this taxing was "first made" when Cyrenius was governor of Syria. Josephus describes the census mentioned in Acts 5:37, and some scholars formerly believed Luke to be confused in his dating. However, according to more recent evidences, it has been concluded that Luke was accurate in his dating and that he correctly used the term "first" in opposition to a second census.

The Roman government conducted the census in an orderly fashion, the head of each family journeying to the town where his family records were kept. Consequently, Joseph left Nazareth, a Galilean village, and journeyed to Bethlehem, a Judean village. David had been born in Bethlehem some 1,000 years prior to this census. Therefore, Joseph, of Davidic lineage, returned with Mary to the home of his ancestor. Although it was not required by law that a wife accompany her husband at the time of the census, Luke indicates that Mary's pregnancy was full-term. Had Joseph neglected her and left her in Nazareth, the townspeople may well have ridiculed her at the birth of the child because all would know the brevity of her marriage. That Luke still refers to Mary as Joseph's "espoused wife" is also noteworthy.

The familiar Christmas story is related in simple details (2:7). The great influx of people left no room for the many travelers. The only place available to Joseph and Mary was in a stable where animals were kept. There Jesus was born. The "swaddling clothes" in which Jesus was wrapped consisted of a large square of material with a strip extending from one corner. The Child was first clothed in the square of material, and the longer strip was then wrapped around Him. How humble a birth! How unassuming an introduction into the world! And yet the Saviour whose birth is related historically to the reign of Augustus, also called saviour, remains the focal point of history.

(2) *The Angelic Announcement, 2:8-14.* The fields around Bethlehem continued to be spotted by the shepherds' flocks as they had been 1,000 years previously in the time of David. An angel, a divine messenger, appeared to the group, and the divine and radiant glory became visible to them. For the third time in the gospel, the command, "Stop fearing," is spoken by an angel (cf. 1:13,30). The simple command was further explained by the angel upon the basis that the fear was to be eliminated because of the presence of joy. The shepherds had feared "a great fear," but the messenger brought "a great joy." This joy is to be all inclusive, its origin based in the birth of the Saviour who is further identified as Christ, the Lord. The Jews had longed for a king such as David had been, and now the divine messenger announced the birth of one identified as the Saviour, born in the city of David.

To satisfy the inquisitive nature of the shepherds, the angel announced a sign even before the question could be asked: they would find a baby wrapped in swaddling clothes and lying in a manger. A third divine manifestation was observed in the presence of the angelic hosts who praised God, saying, "Glory in the highest to God and on earth peace to men of good will." The Roman government incessantly emphasized the *pax Romana,* the Roman peace. The emperor was able to give physical peace from the difficulties and problems created by war, but only God could give spiritual peace within the hearts of men.

(3) *The Shepherds' Visit, 2:15-20.* The divine phenomena which

announced the Saviour's birth uniquely impressed the shepherds; their response was simultaneous. The angelic message and hymn of praise had impressed these common folk who were ably entrenched in Jewish religious teachings. They believed the message and desired instantly to see what God had done in their behalf. Some scholars conjecture that these were special shepherds who had the responsibility of tending the Temple flocks. Only in this way could the orthodox be absolutely sure their offerings were without spot and blemish. The important thing is that the shepherds wished to investigate the matter related to them and to see for themselves the working of God.

Luke described the journey as one made "in haste." The term may mean "to accelerate, to hasten, or to cut across." The logical implication is that the shepherds had no time to travel the ordinary pathways, but rather cut across the fields to reach Bethlehem more quickly. The rapid journey was not disappointing. Arriving in Bethlehem, they found Mary, Joseph, and the baby lodged in a stable just as the angel had indicated. The simple shepherds were the first to receive communication concerning the birth of the Saviour. It is equally noteworthy to remember that these same simple shepherds were the first to proclaim this event to others. If their flocks were tended for the purpose of supplying Temple offerings, then their priority in disclosing the events surrounding the birth of the Saviour becomes even more understandable.

Luke did not reveal the influence of the shepherds' testimony; he simply indicated that the people "wondered at what the shepherds told them." It was Mary who was able to fit this visit and testimony into the eternal scheme of God which she had come to understand partially. It seems as if she kept all these pieces of the puzzle and fitted them together to her own satisfaction and joy. She was left to her thoughts, keeping her secret, anticipating the day when the Saviour would be revealed as God's Son. Meanwhile, the shepherds returned to their simple and routine responsibilities of guarding the flocks. Yet, their lives could never be quite the same; they were glorifying and praising God for all that they had heard and seen.

(4) *The Naming and Temple Ceremonies, 2:21-40.* These ceremonies were routine and kept before the Jew his inevitable and personal obligation to God. Although Jesus had already been recognized as the promised Messiah, Luke here described Him as one who participated in the rites of Moses. The Holy Son of God was to be identified as one of covenant relationship and thus was circumcised on the eighth day to fulfill the requirements of the law. At this time

He was given the name "Jesus," which was the name that Gabriel had commanded to be used prior to the Saviour's conception. The name "Jesus" is the "Joshua" of the Old Testament, meaning "the delivering one." "Jesus" itself means "the Lord (Jehovah) is salvation."

The second ceremony discloses the poverty of Joseph and Mary. Based upon the provisions of Leviticus 12, a mother was regarded as ceremonially unclean for 40 days following the birth of a son. At the end of 40 days two sacrifices were to be offered, a lamb as a burnt offering and a pigeon as a sin offering. However, in the case of poverty, a pigeon could be substituted for the lamb. The poverty of the Saviour's home is revealed by the fact that Joseph and Mary brought two pigeons to satisfy the Levitical requirement. In addition to the offerings previously described, Jesus Himself was presented to God (2:22). This presentation is further explained in the words of 2:23, "Every male that openeth the womb shall be called holy to the Lord." Luke placed emphasis upon the idea that all had been done according to the law. This very statement indicates the completeness with which Jesus was identified with His own people. He too lived under the law, His life a complete obedience to God in conditions common to those of the people whom He had come to serve.

To this point the Temple experiences had been somewhat routine. The newly-born son had been offered to God, and the purification offerings had been made according to the requirements of the law. At this time, however, the experiences of Joseph, Mary, and the baby Jesus became unique within themselves. Simeon (2:25) was described by Luke as a just and devout man who had received a revelation through the Holy Spirit that he would not see death before he had seen the Lord's Christ. At this moment, Simeon was moved by God's Spirit and recognized Jesus as the promised Messiah. He took the small baby in his arms and praised God for all that he had been privileged to witness. Now the Spirit's promise to Simeon had been fulfilled. Simeon insisted that he had seen God's salvation which had been prepared before all the people, the mission of the Saviour itself being spoken of as a light (2:29-32) which would illuminate the Gentiles and also be the glory of Israel. Joseph and Mary marveled at what they saw and heard. Yet, in the midst of their exaltation Simeon introduced for the first time a note of sorrow into the ministry of the Saviour. In his words addressed specifically to Mary, he insisted that the baby was "sent for the rising and falling of many in Israel." Some would find Jesus to be a stumbling block and would fall. Still others would rise because of Him. He is described further as "a sign that is spoken against." This sign will clearly indicate a way to salvation, but many will reject Him and stumble over His person and claims. This one will reveal the true motives of all hearts inasmuch as all men must decide to accept or reject Him. The sorrow, however, did not conclude with this: there is the suggestion that the results of all this would bring sorrow and suffering to Mary's heart (2:35).

Anna, an aged prophetess and the daughter of Phanuel, of the tribe of Aser, added her testimony to that of Simeon. This prophetess, a widow, was approximately 84 years of age. She remained constantly within the Temple area, serving God with prayers and fastings day and night. She also thanked God for His provision of a Saviour and commended the baby Jesus to all who looked for redemption in Jerusalem. This redemption was to culminate in a cross and resurrection experience yet 33 years away. According to Luke's account, the infant Jesus attracted no one except Simeon and Anna. The Temple officials were much too concerned with their positions in administrating the affairs of their glorious institution to attend the needs of a simple couple who had come to offer purification sacrifices occasioned by the birth of a son.

Luke concluded the infancy narratives with the notation that Joseph and Mary performed all the requirements of the Mosaic law and then returned to the village of Nazareth, their home. The actual incarnation of Jesus is explained in Luke 2:40 in words expressive of genuine growth and development. This brief statement records 12 years of Jesus' life. His mental and spiritual development was as genuine as His physical growth. The Child grew (was growing) and waxed strong (was waxing strong). Luke used both of these verbs in 1:80 to describe the growth of John. He added the expression "filled with wisdom," which suggests that the process of mental growth kept pace with physical development. Luke sounded the benediction with the assertion that "the grace of God was upon him."

4. *The Youth of Jesus, 2:41-52.* These verses record the only glimpse into the youth of Jesus, other than the simple statement of 2:40. Although abbreviated, this record does reveal several interesting facts concerning the home in which Jesus was reared. The home was a typically Jewish home; the parents customarily attended the annual Passover feast. In Exodus 23:14 and Deuteronomy 16:16 the Israelites were commanded to participate in the three principal festivals, and it became a common practice for Jews living outside Jerusalem to attend only the Passover. Luke does not indicate whether Jesus had previously attended the Passover along with His parents, but he does

reveal that the young lad accompanied His mother and Joseph to the feast at this particular time. He likely attended this particular feast in order to be prepared for participation the following year when He would be recognized as a member of the community. This participation occurred when the Jewish boy was 13 years of age.

Following the Passover and the Feast of Unleavened Bread (a seven-day period beginning Passover night), Joseph and Mary began their return journey toward Nazareth. Having traveled for one day and having failed to see the child, they began a thorough search (they were searching intensively) but were unable to find Him. Obviously, they had believed Him to be with their kinsmen, but He was nowhere to be found. Having determined that Jesus was not in the company, the parents returned to the Temple, where they found Him.

Jewish students of the law were fond of occupying various courts of the Temple area where they disputed facts and theories pertinent to the scriptures. It was in one of these courts that Jesus had identified Himself with the scholars of His time, listening to their disputes, interrogating them at given points, and at other times answering their questions. This routine procedure was followed by the rabbinical teachers in the instruction of their own disciples. Luke portrays Jesus as a pupil who was seeking to learn from His teachers. His depth and brilliance astonished the rabbis.

Joseph and Mary were equally astonished. The verb means "to strike out or to drive out." In modern parlance one might say, "Their eyes almost popped out of their heads." They had not been aware of His unusual ability. Yet, a mother's love was revealed in the question, "Son, why hast thou thus dealt with us?" Mary admitted her anxious concern and sorrow in the expression, "Behold, thy father and I have sought thee sorrowing." The genuine humanity of the parents expressed itself both in their activity and their questioning. Although an angel had spoken to both prior to Jesus' birth and they were aware of the unusual circumstances surrounding that birth, Joseph and Mary had not fully comprehended the meaning of these experiences. Consequently, Jesus' reply is likewise one of amazement. Jesus apparently expressed surprise in their questioning of where He might be found. It would seem as if He were saying, "Do you not know that there is only one place in Jerusalem for me?" But Mary herself was not prepared to understand all that Jesus said in the reply, "Do you not know that I must be about my Father's business?" The word "business" could better be translated "house." Jesus, at age 12, already possessed an awareness of His peculiar relationship with God. The knowledge of this relationship was to continue to grow and develop during the years to be spent at Nazareth.

Luke concludes this account very simply. Jesus returned to Nazareth, and as an obedient child was subject to His parents. The next 18 years of His life would be spent in Nazareth, where He would develop into manhood and become a carpenter of His village (Mark 6:3). Jesus "was increasing in wisdom and stature and in favor with God and man" (2:52). The expression "was increasing" means literally to cut one's way ahead as a lumberjack hacks his way through the forest. His development—physically, intellectually, and spiritually—was perfect.

These years of obscurity gave Mary additional time to reflect upon the miraculous events surrounding the birth of Jesus. Luke succinctly indicates that she "was keeping these sayings in her heart." There must have existed in Mary an untold story of the cross; for she, as no other individual, had divine revelation concerning the nature of Jesus, His unusual understanding, and His ultimate purpose.

5. *Preparation for the Messiah's Ministry, 3:1-4:15.* The Messiah's birth and youth had now been disclosed by Luke and he turned his pen to the task of describing the formal preparation for the Messiah's ministry. The divine leadership had been revealed in His birth and youth, and now the same divine leadership was to be revealed in the formal preparation for the ministry of the Saviour.

(1) *The Forerunner's Ministry, 3:1-20.* The carefulness of Luke the historian is evidenced by the detailed historical descriptions surrounding the ministry of the forerunner. Luke 3:1 establishes the governmental stage, while 3:2 sets the religious background. In the preface to the gospel, Luke promised Theophilus that his record had been carefully traced from the beginning and that he was writing in order for his reader to have full knowledge of the events in which he had been instructed.

Tiberias had become emperor at the death of Caesar Augustus in A.D. 14. Thus, the fifteenth year of his reign would have been A.D. 28-29. However, some commentators insist that the monarchial reign in Syria was calculated according to a method which had been retained from the days of the Seleucidae. According to this system, the new year began in September. Employing this means of calculation, the fifteenth year of Tiberias might have begun in September-October of A.D. 27. Luke further identified the time by stating that Pontius Pilate was then Governor of Judea; Herod, the Tetrarch of

Galilee; Philip, the Tetrarch of Iturea and Trachonitis; and Lysanias, the Tetrarch of Abilene. Pilate served as procurator of Judea from A.D. 26-36; Herod Antipas (son of Herod the Great) served as Tetrarch of Galilee and Perea from 4 B.C.-A.D. 39; Philip (son of Herod the Great) was Tetrarch of Iturea and Trachonitis from 4 B.C.-A.D. 34; and Lysanias ruled over Abilene, an area to the north of Philip's territory.

Luke, however, was even more detailed by relating these events to the religious leaders. Annas served as high priest from A.D. 6-15, at which time he was removed from office by Gratus, the Roman governor. So far as the Jews were concerned, Annas still retained the priestly power and was extremely influential during the high priesthood of Caiaphas, his son-in-law. The Greek text uses the singular term "priesthood" and not "priesthoods," indicating that the period of the two was actually considered by the historian as one period. In sharp contrast to all the glory and splendor automatically connected with the Jewish priesthood, Luke almost abruptly indicated that the Word of God came unto John, the son of Zacharias, while he was in the wilderness. Contrast the wilderness scene with the Temple scenes, and one immediately confronts the religious situation as it existed in that day. The Temple scenes revealed the toleration of the current religious climate by Rome; the wilderness scene revealed the intolerance of the Jewish religious leaders.

Years, perhaps even centuries, had passed since God's prophetic voice had been heard in Israel. The silence was broken when John came into the region of the Jordan, preaching a "repentance kind of baptism" for the remission of sins. Only after men repented of their sins did John baptize them. This strange preacher viewed himself as the fulfillment of Isaiah's prophecy (40:3); he was the forerunner of the Messiah.

As the roadway was prepared for the monarch who visited a village, even so it was John's responsibility to prepare spiritually the way over which the Lord would travel. The hill was to be lowered, while the valley was to be filled. The crooked roadway was to be straightened, and the rough ways smoothed. The Jews believed that prophecy would reappear with the coming of the Messianic Age (Joel 2:28; Malachi 3:1). John's role was more than merely prophetic. He was an integral part of his world's moving toward the coming of the kingdom. John, as the herald of Jesus, called for a radical change described by the term "repentance." But his message did not end at this point; his was a message essential to the preparation of the world for the coming of the Messiah. Obstacles were to be removed before the Lord came. All of history had moved and was moving in the direction of the coming of the kingdom.

Many people from various walks of life responded to the proclamation of John. This preparer, who could never be praised for his tact or diplomacy, addressed some of his hearers as a "generation of vipers." Matthew 3:7 indicates that these words were descriptive of the Pharisees and Sadducees. This harsh address illumined the self-satisfaction of the group and the fact that they sought protection from judgment without an alteration of life. John called men to a genuine repentance, a repentance which discloses itself in the alteration of life. Instead of rushing as vipers before fire, men were to alter their lives by repentance. When man repents, he does "an about face," he walks in the opposite direction, he aligns himself with God. His mere sorrow can never be described as repentance. One of the most serious obstacles to the Jews' repentance was their proclivity to claim kinship to Abraham. John stated that God did not simply desire men related to Abraham. Were this nationalistic conclave all that He desired, God could raise children to Abraham from the stones at the forerunner's feet. Repentance was imperative!

Even then the ax was being laid to the root of the trees. Each tree which brought forth bad fruit was cut down and was cast into the fire. The urgency of these words prompted people to inquire of John concerning their obligations. John insisted that repentance is manifested in life. Repentance was revealed in the lives of those who possessed an excess of food and clothing by their sharing with the less fortunate. Integrity and personal honesty with which they collected their taxes and discharged their responsibilities evidenced repentance in the lives of tax collectors and soldiers. Tax collectors were hated by the Jews, but a penitent tax collector could perform his responsibility in an honest manner. John instructed the soldiers to deal justly and never accuse men falsely. The soldiers of John's day often supplemented their salaries either by fraud or by the threat of violence. John left no possibility that his hearers might misinterpret the message of repentance. He insisted that a man's entering into the kingdom expressed itself in an ethical and moral relationship to his fellow man.

This prophetic proclamation (3:15) created excitement and expectation in the hearts of John's hearers. This significant question remained: Is this the Christ? Perhaps a second question followed closely. Are messianic hopes again to be dashed to the ground? John quickly allayed their fears and guided their interpretation of his person. He recognized the importance and significance of his preparatory work; but he insisted that his baptism was a water baptism, the only baptism he could administer. He acknowledged that the One coming would be greater, so great that he was unworthy even to loosen the strings of His sandals—the task assigned to the lowest slave in the household. This One who was to follow was to baptize "with the Holy Spirit and with fire."

Fire is destructive, but in that sense it is also a cleansing agent. The saturation of one's personality with the Holy Spirit suggested a cleansing and purification. This suggestion of purification is emphasized additionally in the illustration of the threshing floor. John pictured the farmer as he separated the chaff from the wheat, the wheat being gathered into the granary and the chaff burned with fire. The Messiah's coming would not mean salvation for all; the good would be separated from the bad. The impenitent would be destroyed; the coming of the kingdom would enact a great separation.

Luke (3:18) indicated that John's message included other exhortations, but these proclamations were left undefined. However, the important aspect of the message had been defined. The appearance of the Messiah was to bring a radical separation, the unrepentant being separated from those whose hearts had been cleansed internally by the working of God's Spirit. Josephus describes the ministry of the forerunner, his imprisonment; and subsequent death (*Antiquities* 18, 52).

(2) *The Messiah's Baptism, 3:21-22.* A more detailed picture of Jesus' baptism is recorded in Matthew 3:16-17 and Mark 1:9-11. Luke makes no reference to John's initial refusal to baptize Jesus, nor does he explain John's conviction that he should be baptized by Jesus. His years of perfect growth and maturity (cf. 2:52) had now culminated in His baptismal experience. Jesus (3:21) was not among the first to be baptized by John, and Luke adds that many people had already submitted to John's baptism. The multitudes had been baptized because of repentance (3:3), but Jesus had no sin of which to repent (cf. II Corinthians 5:21; Hebrews 4:15; I Peter 2:22). The Suffering Servant passage of Isaiah 53 pictured clearly the fact that Jesus was bearing the sins for the many. In the first public act of the Saviour's ministry, Jesus identified Himself with the people whom He had come to save. This identification was effected through His baptism. From the inception of His public ministry, Jesus headed toward the cross, a direction further established in the temptation (4:1-13).

The Matthean account suggests that baptism was necessary for the fulfillment of righteousness, and Jesus as a righteous Jew subjected Himself to John's baptism. By so doing He became one with the people for whom He would die.

In His baptism heaven was opened to Him, disclosing that in a unique way Jesus was able to observe God's glory and majesty. God's acceptance of Jesus' baptism and identification was further defined in the descent of the Holy Spirit, who descended in the form of a dove. Luke does not indicate that a dove actually was present, but states that the Spirit came as a dove. The undeniable and important fact is that the Spirit came upon Jesus. This does not mean that Jesus had not previously enjoyed the Spirit's presence, but that the Spirit came upon Him in a new way. He was now equipped to inaugurate His public ministry. Still another sign of God's acceptance was evidenced in the voice which said, "Thou art my beloved Son; in thee I am well pleased." God declared Jesus to be His eternal Son and placed His stamp of approval upon the action of Jesus. For 30 years He had lived as a perfect man. Now the perfect Son had identified Himself totally and completely with His eternal mission. Jesus was ready to begin the long journey which would culminate in victory over sin.

(3) *The Master's Genealogy, 3:23-38.* Before introducing the public ministry of Jesus, Luke relegated all else to the background and established Jesus as the central personality in the following account. Therefore, it was logical that he would begin by establishing the genealogy of Jesus. The genealogical record is introduced by a reference to the age of Jesus (3:23). Having stated, Jesus' age, he acknowledged the common supposition concerning Jesus' identity, stating that people "supposed" Jesus to be the son of Joseph.

The genealogy presents many difficulties. The Jews were interested in genealogical records—primarily because of lessons learned from the Exile experiences and the records' importance to priestly orders. However, this particular record poses problems. The Old Testament contains many genealogical records. The fact that Luke recorded the genealogy poses no problem, but the manner in which it was recorded does create questions. People of Davidic descent would have been particularly cautious in recording their genealogical tables because the Old Testament spoke of the Messiah as coming from the house of David. Luke probably received his information of the table from Mary. It was not customary to insert a woman's name into a genealogical table; therefore, Joseph's name was substituted for Mary's name. Luke was meticulous and specific in stating that Jesus was the "supposed" son of Joseph. The insertion of Joseph's name created no problem for Luke, for in earlier sections he had carefully stated that Joseph was not the father of the Saviour.

When this genealogy is compared with the one in Matthew (1:1-17), obvious differences are noted. Matthew gives the genealogy of Joseph. He was writing to meet the needs of Jews, and his basic thesis was to prove that Jesus was the Messiah. Although the Saviour had no earthly father, Joseph was recognized as the legal father and was himself of Davidic descent. On the other hand, Luke wrote to meet the needs of the world. He purposed to present Jesus as the Universal Saviour. If Jesus was to be the Universal Saviour, then He must be presented as one identified universally with the race. His purpose did not touch merely the Jew, but included all men. The focal point of history is not reached in His relationship to the Jew, but in His relationship to humanity. As Saviour of all men, He was to touch all men.

In Matthew's discussion of the events prior to the birth of Jesus, his material is organized around Joseph and his reactions. Luke gives his attention to Mary and her experiences with Gabriel and Elizabeth. The universal nature of Jesus' ministry is established in the genealogical record, illustrated in the ministries recorded by Luke, and conclusively stated in the words "that repentance and remission of sins should be preached in his name among all nations, beginning at Jerusalem" (24:47).

(4) *The Messiah's Temptation, 4:1-13.* Some interpreters minimize the temptation of Jesus, attempting to explain that He was involved in a mock battle. To appreciate Luke's account of Jesus' temptation, one must remember that this is not the record of a straw man's battle, nor was the temptation a mock battle. The temptation of Jesus is recorded not only in the synoptics, but the author of the epistle to the Hebrews emphasized the fact that Jesus was tempted. The author suggested (2:18) that "he himself had suffered being tempted. . . ." He further stated (4:15) that Jesus "was in all points tempted like as we are. . . ." Therefore, the temptation of Jesus was as genuine, severe, and complete as that of modern man. He would not have been capable of sympathy nor understanding apart from subjection to the experiences common to humanity. Because Jesus suffered temptation, He is able to "suffer with us, whenever temptation comes."

The temptation of Jesus must not be limited to the wilderness experience. If He was tempted in all points as modern man is tempted, then His temptation could never be limited to the wilderness area. Luke indicates (4:13) that the devil "departed from him for a season." Satan returned at numerous intervals during the earthly ministry of Jesus, two classic examples being when the people wished to make Jesus their king by force (John 6:15) and the Gethsemane experience (Mark 14:32-41). Perhaps as in no other aspect of Jesus' activity, the temptation experience defined the character of His Messiahship. In this experience Jesus had opportunity to choose an easy way to public acceptance, but He spoke only in terms of dedication to God's will. This dedication to God's eternal purpose would unquestionably evolve into a difficult road culminating in the cross.

During the wilderness temptation, Jesus was invited to become king of the world by denying His relationship to the Father. The temptation of Jesus must always be remembered as a part of the endless struggle between the devil and God.

Luke describes Jesus as filled with the Spirit following the baptism experience and as being directed by the Spirit into the wilderness area. The wilderness area is left undefined by Luke, but it may be assumed to have been in the Jordan area. The temptations extended over a period of 40 days. The first temptation revolved around personal preservation. After Jesus had fasted for 40 days, the devil said, "Since you are a Son of God, say to this stone that it might become bread." To understand that Satan did not approach Jesus at a weak point, but at one of His strongest convictions, is important. At the time of Jesus' baptism, the voice from heaven had declared Jesus to be God's beloved Son. Perhaps the devil sought to create dissatisfaction by suggesting that God should never treat His Son in this fashion. Jesus had already accepted God's purpose for His life; and if He was sure of one thing, it was His Sonship. The Saviour's response to this temptation was one of finality and definiteness. God's Spirit had guided Him into the wilderness; He could never question the Father's love for the Son. The Saviour's familiarity with the Old Testament provided His recourse. Using the words of Deuteronomy 8:3, He replied that "man shall not live by bread alone, but by every word of God." These words suggest that man is dependent upon God in every responsibility and aspect of life. God, who had nourished the Israelites with manna and quail, could surely supply the wilderness needs of His Son. He totally committed Himself to God's purpose and did not yield to the temptation of self-preservation.

The second temptation originated with man's common desire for power and prestige. Luke indicates (4:5) that the devil took Jesus into a high mountain from which He could view the kingdoms of the world in a fleeting moment. The panoramic view of the kingdoms in their glory occurred in a "point of time." The temptation becomes more meaningful when one remembers that Satan had knowledge of the messianic kingdom and knew that Jesus had come for the purpose of establishing it. His suggestion evolves around the Saviour's worship. If Jesus would worship Satan and thereby recognize his authority, Jesus would receive not simply a messianic kingdom, but all the kingdoms of the world. Satan's deceit is revealed in the promise, and it must be remembered that Jesus Himself spoke of the devil as a prince of this world (John 12:31, 14:30, 16:11). Jesus meant that Satan ruled the world in the sense that sin ruled within the hearts of the world's leaders. Jesus foiled the devil's intent a second time. He refused to accept the current Jewish idea of the Messiah as an earthly ruler. Again His answer was based upon the Old Testament's warning in Deuteronomy 6:13, "Thou shalt worship the Lord thy God, and him only shalt thou serve." As He would later teach in the Sermon on the Mount (Matthew 6:24), in this moment of temptation Jesus recognized that man cannot worship God and Satan. The commandment insists upon God's worship. The absoluteness of God's Word is clearly underscored in Jesus' willingness to live by its precepts.

The third temptation occurred with Jesus on a pinnacle of the Temple (perhaps in thought as was the former temptation), the temptation itself attacking a strong point. The Greek construction could be translated, "Since you are the Son of God . . ." Employing the words of Psalm 91:11-12, Satan rationalized this temptation: "He shall give his angels charge over thee, to keep thee: and in their hands they shall bear thee up, lest at any time thou dash thy foot against a stone." Erroneously interpreted and applied, these words suggested that Jesus would have been correct in assuming that God would protect Him regardless of His vain and idle tempting of God. Satan, employing words which the rabbis interpreted as referring directly to the Messiah, suggested that the logical thing for one who wished to become the Messiah was to cast Himself from the pinnacle into the midst of His people, who even then had joined in the hour of prayer. Perhaps at this very time they were praying for the coming of the Messiah. He would then have been received with open arms, and the road of suffering could have been avoided. For the third time, Jesus repelled the temptation by depending upon a teaching from Deuteronomy 6:16, "You will not tempt (test, try, determine how far

He will go) the Lord your God." This temptation at the point of the spectacular self-display was not compatible with God's will for Him. To test God, to see how far one can "push" Him, is not to trust Him.

The temptations as a formal trial had now ended. Jesus had been tempted from the standpoint of self-preservation, power, and spectacular self-display. During the forty-day period, Jesus had been subjected to relentless tempting, and likely these three are but typical of all that occurred during the longer period. Luke alone records the fact that Satan left for a time after having completed every temptation. He was to return in the desire of the masses who would take Jesus forcibly and name Him political king and even more dramatically in the person of Simon Peter during Jesus' last hours.

(5) *The Messiah's Subsequent Fame, 4:14-15.* Luke does not complete the story of Jesus' ministry following the temptation but rather follows the general outline of Mark and records His return to Galilee. Yet, the author is precise in stating that He returned to Galilee in the Spirit's power. The term "power" is the word from which the English "dynamite" is derived. These brief words summarize the Galilean ministry as being enacted in the power of the Spirit, as revolving around the synagogue activities, and as being a time of fame for the Saviour. The word "fame" is derived from a verb which means "to say." In contrast to His fame, which continued to spread, Jesus remained involved in the teaching ministries of the synagogues. He was being glorified by all men. The terms "being glorified" are from a verb "to glorify," from which the English word "doxology" is derived. At this point, it would seem that even some of the Jewish religious leaders marveled at His teaching, although some had come already to the point of depreciating and ridiculing him.

FOR FURTHER STUDY

1. Read the article entitled "Nazarite" in *The Interpreter's Dictionary of the Bible,* p. 526.
2. Read J. Gresham Machen's *The Virgin Birth,* pp. 119-168, for an exhaustive treatment of the Lucan narrative.
3. Read the article entitled "John the Baptist" in *The Zondervan Pictorial Bible Dictionary,* pp. 438-439.
4. What were the current Jewish conceptions of Messiahship? How did John's ministry elicit favorable response in light of these? How did John's ministry differ from popular Jewish conceptions? Cf. H. E. Dana, *The New Testament World,* pp. 131-139.
5. Using an exhaustive concordance, compare the synoptic references to the Messiah.

PART II

The Galilean Ministry

CHAPTER THREE

From the Rejection in Nazareth to the Choice of the Twelve

The extensive Galilean ministry is described by Luke in 4:14-9:50. Comparison with the Marcan account indicates the independence of the gospel writers. The events recorded in Mark 6:45-8:26 do not appear in Luke's record, nor did Mark record the events of Luke 6:20-8:4. Comparison with the Marcan account further reveals that Luke gives a more complete account while Mark writes in terse and abbreviated fashion.

1. *Rejection at Nazareth, 4:16-30.* In 4:14-15, Luke describes briefly the Galilean ministry of Jesus and reveals that this ministry brought unprecedented popularity to the Saviour. He was glorified as a teacher even in the synagogues, the stronghold of the Pharisees and the "grass roots" of Judaism. This passage under consideration records the experiences of Jesus at Nazareth and is both incisive and instructive. Nazareth was His home, and there He had worked in Joseph's carpenter shop. Jesus, as a good Jew, went to the synagogue on the Sabbath. To attend the synagogue services was His custom. The synagogue was likely the most influential institution in Nazareth. It had originated during the Exile when the Jews were separated from Jerusalem and its Temple services. By the time of Jesus, the synagogue was not only a religious institution but likewise an educational institution, as well as one which served a judicial function.

The synagogue service consisted of numerous benedictions, a selection from the law, a reading of a passage from the prophets, etc.

A visiting rabbi might logically be expected to conduct a portion of the worship service. This home-town boy was selected as the reader of the second passage. He chose Isaiah 61:1-2, a passage picturing the deliverance of Israel from Babylon in the terminology of their Year of Jubilee. In the Year of Jubilee all debts were cancelled, slaves gained their freedom, and all property reverted to the original owners (Leviticus 25). This was a time of "good news" to the poor; the release from captivity would be "good news." The exiles could then happily return to their homeland.

Having stood and read this passage, Jesus rolled the scroll, gave it to the minister of the synagogue (the servant who cared for the synagogue properties), and then sat down. The Greek text indicates that all eyes were "gazing intently" at Him. The eyes did not gaze long, nor did the people question extensively before Jesus pointedly announced the fulfillment of the passage. He affirmed that He had been anointed with the Spirit to proclaim the Gospel to the broken-hearted. Slowly His claim registered with the people. "Is not this Joseph's son?" The question is so stated as to expect an affirmative answer. Jesus did not stop to answer the question, nor to correct their mistake. Rather, He quoted a pithy proverb. "Physician, heal thyself." It was only logical that His hearers would insist that He perform some of the works in His own country that He had performed in Capernaum, the center of His Galilean ministry. These folk were prejudiced and biased against Him personally, and He explained their prejudice in 4:24, "No prophet is accepted in his own country." To prove the truthfulness of His word He referred to Elijah and Elisha who, rejected by their countrymen, ultimately offered God's message and power to the woman of Sidon and to Naaman, the Syrian. This, however, was too much for the Nazarenes to accept.

His sympathetic hearers quickly became hateful enemies. Jesus had insulted them as Hebrews; and even more, He had cast reproach upon His own city. Filled with boiling anger, they drove Him out of the city and intended to cast Him from the hill. Perhaps others guilty of defaming their city or blaspheming their God had been cast from this cliff. But in God's plan for the Universal Saviour the time of death had not arrived. Jesus passed through the teeming mob and returned to Capernaum, where He continued His teaching (cf. 4:16, 30). Luke concludes the account with the observation that all were astonished by His teaching because His word was with power.

2. *Capernaum Ministry, 4:31-44.* Capernaum, a town on the northwestern shore of the Sea of Galilee, became the headquarters of

Jesus' Galilean ministry. Capernaum was located in the region of Zebulun and Naphtali and was obviously a Roman military post (cf. 7:1-10). Because of Jesus' early removal from Nazareth to Capernaum, the latter came to be called His own city (Matthew 9:1; Mark 2:1). Jesus' habit in attending the synagogue services is recounted again in 4:33. One assumes that Jesus had concluded His time of instruction when a man possessed of a demon became the demon's spokesman and cried, "Let us alone; what have we to do with thee, thou Jesus of Nazareth?" Although some interpreters explain demon possession as psychological disturbance, Jesus obviously dealt with the demon-possessed in such manner as to acknowledge demon possession and seemingly expected His disciples to do the same. That the New Testament writers believed in demons cannot be questioned. Even a superficial reading of the gospel materials indicates that the writers distinguished between physical illness and demon possession. In the latter part of this chapter (4:40) Luke carefully distinguishes between the healing of diseased bodies and (4:41) the exorcising of demons. Some commentators argue that Jesus was simply accommodating Himself to the superstitious beliefs of His day; however, this is unlikely. In the Johannine account of Jesus' contact with the man born blind, John (9:1-3) indicates Jesus carefully explained the reason for the man's blindness. Furthermore, when Jesus was accused of casting out demons by Beelzebub, the prince of demons, He did not explain that this was simply illness, not demon possession. To acknowledge that Jesus dealt with demons and in no manner attempted to disclaim their existence seems a logical interpretation of the perplexing problem.

The demon who controlled this man recognized Jesus as "the Holy One of God." Luke recorded no dialogue or argument, merely indicating that Jesus rebuked the demon and commanded him to come out of the man. The command literally is constituted by the words, "Be muzzled and come out from him." In his strength and rage the demon threw the man to the ground, but departed without injuring the victim. This surprising manifestation of Jesus' power amazed the people, who began to discuss the event. What kind of man could command demons? Luke concludes the account with a simple reference to the fact that His fame was widespread.

This power over the spiritual and physical aspect of man is further illustrated in His total ability to heal the sick. Having left the synagogue, He went to the home of Simon Peter. Simon's mother-in-law was extremely ill, her fever described as "great." Luke discloses the seriousness of her condition, and then emphasizes the simplicity of Jesus' miracle with the notation that He "rebuked the fever, and it left her." Although an intense fever invariably weakens the body, her healing was a complete restoration. This completeness can be seen in the expression, ". . . immediately she arose and continued ministering to them."

The Saviour's growing fame and the account of His healing many who were brought to Him are revealed in 4:40-44. A Jew would not carry a burden on a Sabbath, and Luke is careful to indicate the Sabbath had concluded when those with various diseases were brought to the Master. The expression "when the sun was setting" indicates that the Sabbath had passed, inasmuch as the Jew reckoned the beginning and ending of a day with the setting of the sun. The diseases were numerous, and the sick were many. Yet, Jesus laid His hands on each and healed all their infirmities. Furthermore, Jesus again exorcised demons; these demons recognized Jesus and properly evaluated Him as the Christ (4:41). The tenderness of the Master changed to sternness when He dealt with the demons. He did not permit them to speak. Jesus dared not receive the testimony of the devil's envoy. Not only did He have the power to exorcise the demon, He also had the power to prevent his speaking.

Early the next morning, Jesus left Galilee and went into a desert area. Perhaps this gives an insight into His true humanity. Jesus was tired and weary after a night of healing, but He was unable to find refuge. The people "were seeking" Him, eventually found Him, and begged Him not to leave Capernaum. However, He indicated that He was morally (*dei*) obligated to preach the kingdom to other cities. This was His commission. The term translated, "I must," is a Greek word which carries with it the idea of moral necessity. It is the same word employed by Jesus in His conversation with Nicodemus: "Marvel not that I say that you must be born again. . . ." The Galilean tour harmonized with the expressed purpose of Jesus' ministry. It is worthy of note that the synagogue became the primary base of operation for Jesus' public ministry.

3. *Diversified Teachings and Miraculous Healings, 5:1-6:11.* This entire section is composed of the accounts of numerous teachings and healings performed by Jesus. For the most part, these are brief accounts separated from similar teachings and miracles by the records of the choosing of the Twelve and the Sermon on the Plain. Luke has concluded the previous account by showing the necessity of Jesus' preaching in other cities. The Master Himself

insisted that He would not be simply a miracle worker or an exorciser of demons. He had come to preach the kingdom of God and this He must do. However, He was never able to forego the personal needs of man.

(1) *Teaching on the Sea and Calling Four Disciples, 5:1-11.* The beautiful Sea of Galilee served often as the scene of Jesus' ministry. From its waters or its shores Jesus gave some of the supreme teachings of His ministry. On this occasion the broad shores of the Sea of Galilee (Lake of Gennesaret) served as His pulpit. The people pressed against Him (the same verb is used in John 11:38 to describe the resting of a stone on the tomb, and in John 21:9 to describe the fish on the coals), and the only way to maintain a desirable teaching situation was for Jesus to enter a boat, leaving the crowds on the shore. Two ships were near, and the fishermen were engaged in washing the heavy nets. Jesus chose Simon's ship and requested that he push out from the shore.

The author moves quickly from the teaching account to the call of the four disciples. When Jesus had finished His teaching ministry, He told Simon to move the ship into deeper water and there cast his nets. The expert fisherman, who was familiar with every nook and cranny of the lake, insisted it was futile to cast the nets. He and his partners had toiled unsuccessfully throughout the night. Weary from hours of lifting and dragging the nets, he nevertheless acquiesced to the word of the Master. His confidence in the word of Jesus was rewarded by such a large catch of fish that the net began to tear, and his partners came to assist in hauling the loaded net into the ship. The catch proved to be even more than Simon had anticipated, for both ships were filled to the point of sinking. These professional fishermen were impressed by the word of Jesus, but it was Simon who expressed their genuine feelings. His statement, "Depart from me; for I am a sinful man, O Lord," suggests the great gulf which separated Jesus from the ordinary man. Here God incarnate was identified with man; but in His miraculous power there was evidenced immediately a vast difference between Jesus and His followers.

Peter had observed previous revelations of Jesus' power, but the present revelation dramatically impressed all who observed. James and John, sons of Zebedee, were equally impressed with what they had observed; these men were partners of Peter (5:10). The prohibition, "Stop fearing," which had been spoken on numerous other occasions, was once again repeated. Jesus revealed that He would change their vocations and henceforth they would catch men. Perhaps

Simon Peter did not fully realize the connotation of these terms until the Pentecost experience.

Luke concludes his account by indicating the finality with which these men forsook all to follow Jesus. A deeper meaning is to be seen in this experience. The Jesus who demanded discipleship is the Jesus who promised provision to those who are His followers. If Jesus could provide a miraculous draught of fishes, He could surely supply whatever Peter, his friends, and their loved ones needed.

(2) *Healing the Leper and the Paralytic, 5:12-26.* The Jews viewed leprosy as a sign of moral uncleanness as well as a disease (Numbers 12; II Kings 5:19-27; II Chronicles 26:16-21). Lepers were separated from society, not only as a hygienic measure but also as a sign of separation from fellowship with God's people. Their lives were exceedingly miserable, and they depended either upon receiving alms or scavenging for a living. They sometimes went about in groups (17:12). This man's disease was in the advanced stages; the notation of this fact discloses the author's interest in the man's medical condition. The leper fell on his face, not demanding a cure but stating, "Lord, if you will, you are able to cleanse me." Jewish social custom forbade a leper to walk on the roadway, insisting that the leper must walk alongside the roadway, constantly crying, "Unclean, unclean!" lest someone should touch him and thereby become contaminated. Jesus, however, put His hand on the leper's body and replied, "I will, be cleansed." The leprosy immediately left its victim. The adverb employed suggests that the cure was instantaneous. By touching the leper, Jesus indicated that no man was to be eliminated from His fellowship. His commandment to the cleansed man was threefold: (1) Tell no one what had occurred. At this stage of His ministry, Jesus did not wish to attract men by His miracles but desired that they might be attracted by His word. (2) Show himself to the priest. This was a part of the law specified in Leviticus 13. (3) Offer the sacrifices according to the law. The appropriate offerings are defined in Leviticus 14.

The cleansed man (Mark 1:45) did not obey Jesus and related widely the miracle of cleansing. This report increased the crowds; perhaps also increased was the temptation of Jesus to accept their plaudits and to reject the purpose of the cross. The reference in 5:17 seems simply to record the presence of Pharisees and scribes who had assembled to hear Jesus and observe His miracles. Yet in practical effect, their apparent innocence was not realistic. Men of this character would later attack Jesus because of His violations of rabbinical Sabbath law and thereby question His integrity and intent.

The healing of the paralytic is also described in Mark 2:3 ff., and Matthew 9:2 ff. Four men had such faith in Jesus that they decided to bring their palsied friend to Him. However, so many people had surrounded the house that they could not bring him through the doorway. Their strong faith prompted them to climb to the housetop, open the roof, and lower the palsied friend on a couch. In this healing miracle, Jesus was proclaiming the fact that He had the authority to heal spiritually as well as physically. The scribes (professional interpreters of the law) and the Pharisees reasoned that Jesus spoke blasphemously. All Jews agreed that God alone could forgive sin. Jesus, aware of their doubts and accusations, inquired: "Which is easier to say, Thy sins be forgiven thee, or Rise up and walk?" Forgiveness of sin could not be proved or disproved; therefore, Jesus said to the palsied man, "Arise, and take up thy couch, and go into thine house." The instantaneous healing is described by the expression "Immediately he rose . . . took up that upon which he lay . . . and departed. . . ." As the man left for his own dwelling, he "kept glorifying" God. The scribes and Pharisees had been correct in stating that God alone could forgive sin; they had been incorrect in their interpretation of the person of Jesus.

(3) *Calling a Tax Collector to Discipleship, 5:27-32.* The brief account of Matthew's call to discipleship sometimes prompts the interpreter to overlook the significance of the action. His place in Jewish society was one of scorn and reproach. To collect customs on the goods transported on the main road between Acre and Damascus was his responsibility. The practices of men such as Matthew earned them a social position of reproach and contempt. It seems as if the publicans had no established tax and could therefore levy a tax on the goods, the animal drawing the cart, the cart itself, or even the cart's wheels. Such practices had made them extremely wealthy. Levi, also called Matthew (Matthew 9:9), was sitting at a place of taxation when Jesus came and commanded him "to follow." The command is a present tense; the simple response was expressed in such fashion as to indicate that he left all decisively and "was following" Jesus (imperfect tense).

Just to follow Jesus was hardly enough to satisfy Matthew. Having found a new master, he wished to introduce Him to his friends. However, his circle of friends would never have been condoned by fellow Jews. Yet, Jesus accepted Matthew's invitation to attend a great feast in His honor. The scribes and Pharisees were murmuring (buzzing as bees) concerning Jesus' social contact with the publicans and sinners. The scribes and Pharisees were likely uninvited; but probably by this time they took every opportunity to gather evidence against Jesus, even to the point of becoming uninvited "guests." Here they found Jesus eating at the same table with publicans and sinners, an evidence that He accepted their fellowship. These tax collectors were placed in the same category as the man who disobeyed God's moral law. Jesus' answer to the accusation brought against Him was very simple. Only sick folk need a physician. His ministry was to call sinners to repentance. Only sinners needed to change attitudes, character, mind, and life.

(4) *Teachings Concerning the Nature of His Religion, 5:33-39.* These verses record two events which elucidate and illustrate the nature of Jesus' religion. The first is a question occasioned by the fasting of John's disciples and the continued normalcy of Jesus' followers. Fasting was very important in Judaism and was usually followed by prayer. Pharisees customarily fasted twice during the week (18:12). Instead of fasting as did John's disciples, the followers of Jesus led a normal life. The Master's answer to the question relative to fasting revolves around a social custom of the day. Life was generally difficult for a young Jew, and the week of his marriage was the happiest week of his life. In those days, the young couple invited their close friends to spend this week with them. These guests were called "the children of the bridechamber." The rabbis had relieved the young bride and groom, along with the children of the bridechamber, of some of the religious responsibilities which might lessen their joy during the week. It was not necessary for them to fast or to observe certain other religious practices during this week. Using this as a background, Jesus answered the question with another question: Why should the children of the bridechamber fast while the bridegroom is with them? Yet the days will come when the Bridegroom (Christ) will be taken from them, and then His followers will fast. This is Jesus' first reference to His approaching death.

The second teaching of Jesus concerning the nature of His religion is seen in the parable of the new patch on an old garment. This parable also illustrates the extreme difference between Judaism and the religion introduced by Jesus. To patch an old garment with a piece of new material is foolish; for a Jew to insist that Jesus' way of life was simply a "new patch" on Judaism is equally senseless. A second parable, that of the wineskin, is even more expressive. Wine was stored in bottles made from the skins of small animals. When these skins became old, they became brittle and broke easily. Jesus suggested that no man puts new wine into an old bottle because the new wine is still fermenting. The fermentation would cause the brittle skins to burst and the wine would then spill, the bottles also perishing. The Jew could not take the principles and precepts of Jesus and force them into the old forms of Judaism. Although the Jew regarded fasting as a superior expression of dedication, fasting was not so regarded by Jesus. He concluded this teaching with the suggestion that the individual who has drunk old wine does not immediately desire new wine inasmuch as he feels the old is superior. Even as new patches were obvious on old garments and new wine burst old wineskins, so the coming of the Saviour brought such radical change that His religion must find new methods of expression.

(5) *Teachings Concerning the Sabbath, 6:1-11*. In the preceding passage Jesus revealed His departure from the forms of Judaism. These forms were totally inadequate to contain and express all that Jesus brought. In 6:1-11, Jesus applies His previous statement to the law of the Sabbath. The Sabbath reminded the Jews weekly that God had created the world and also that He had redeemed them from their Egyptian bondage. The Sabbath was to be a day holy to God (Exodus 20:10). The Sabbath law had been given for the purpose of glorifying God. To glorify God on the Sabbath meant that one would cease his labors. The interpretation of the Sabbath law had created many problems for the Jews, but they had sought to deal minutely with these problems of interpretation. For example, the scribes had determined what constituted work on the Sabbath and what constituted burden bearing. Work had been divided into 39 categories, each category being further divided for interpretative purposes. To honor the Sabbath, one must remember all these specific rules concerning it.

The law prohibited harvesting on the Sabbath (Exodus 34:21). When Jesus and His disciples walked through the grain fields on a particular Sabbath, His disciples innocently plucked the heads of grain, threshing the grain from the chaff by rubbing the heads between their hands. The Pharisees immediately accused them of breaking the Sabbath law. Jesus replied that His disciples had not broken the Sabbath law and referred the Pharisees to the act of David when he and his followers ate the shewbread. It was unlawful for one other than a priest to eat the shewbread; but David, the great hero of the past, led his men in eating shewbread when it became simply a matter of preserving the body. This logic seems to follow: "What was right for David must be right for my disciples." David had employed the higher law of human need in preference to the ceremonial law.

The Messiah was David's Son. In justifying the action of his disciples, Jesus stated in essence that He was David's Son and therefore had the right to do anything that David had done. At this point, Jesus claimed for the Son of Man lordship of the Sabbath. Jesus then made the Sabbath not a day of dread and fear, but a day in which He Himself served as Lord and thereby brought joy and peace to the heart of the worshiper. Jesus insisted that proper Sabbath observance is not related to the minutiae of rules and regulations, but to the lordship of Christ.

Luke further illustrates the lordship of Jesus in the Master's willingness to heal on the Sabbath. On this particular Sabbath, a man with a withered hand was present. Since he was a physician and would be prone to note such details, Luke stated that it was the man's right hand which was withered. The scribes and Pharisees, the watchdogs of religious orthodoxy, closely scrutinized Jesus to determine whether He would heal on the Sabbath. If He healed this man on the Sabbath, this would be one additional accusation to hurl against Jesus. The omniscience of the Lord was revealed in His awareness of their evil disposition. He commanded the man to stand in the midst of the group. While the man stood, Jesus asked whether it was right on the Sabbath to do good or to do evil, and whether it was proper to save life or to destroy it. It goes without saying that the hand had been withered for a long period and the man was in no immediate danger of death. Yet, Jesus straightforwardly violated the ceremonial law and answered His own question by commanding the man to stretch out his hand. The Greek construction seems to indicate that the man stretched out his hand; and when he did, it was made complete as the other. The scribes and Pharisees were not impressed with what they observed, but were filled with an insane rage, a "lack of mind." The Pharisees immediately joined hands with the Herodians in an attempt to destroy the Saviour (Mark 3:6).

4. *Choice of the Twelve, 6:12-19.* Luke's record to this juncture is concerned with the revelation of Jesus as the Son of God and with His divine power. The scene is shifted temporarily from His teaching and miracle working to the selection of His apostles. Little or no background for the selection is given; they were selected during "those days." Obviously the time relationship connects this experience to that of the Sabbath controversies. The importance of the selection

is readily seen in the fact that preparatory to choosing the Twelve, Jesus went into a mountain, where he continued throughout the night in prayer. That Jesus needed the Father's guidance is evident, although the finite mind has difficulty in comprehending the omniscience of Jesus and still greater difficulty in attempting to harmonize His omniscience and human limitation.

With the dawning of a new day, Jesus was prepared to select His apostles. Having assembled His disciples, He then chose 12 whom He named apostles. A "disciple" is a learner or follower, while an "apostle" is one commissioned with a message. One might be a disciple without being an apostle, but one could not be an apostle without first being a learner or follower. Included in the group were all types of men: fishermen, a tax collector, a Zealot, one destined to become a traitor, Galileans, a Judean, tempestuous, kind, loving, leaders, followers, men of faith, and at least one who was eventually to have serious doubt. To such a representative collection as this Jesus would entrust the message of redemption.

When he again came down to the plain, a great multitude of people surrounded Jesus and His disciples. They had come to hear His words, to enjoy the blessings of His healing, to experience the exorcising of their demons, and to know His brief touch. All were seeking to touch Him (6:19). In 6:17-19, Luke introduces the Sermon on the Plain.

For Further Study

1. Check a relief map of Palestine and relate important geographical sites.
2. Read the articles entitled "Nazareth" and "Capernaum" in *The Zondervan Pictorial Bible Dictionary*, pp. 146, 573.
3. Read pp. 336-338 in William Barclay's *The Gospel of Matthew*, Vol. 1, for an excellent discussion of Roman taxation.
4. Research the disease of leprosy, employing biblical references, Bible dictionaries, and a current medical dictionary.
5. Read William Barclay's *The Master's Men* or Gaston Foote's *Meet the Twelve* for helpful discussions of the Twelve Apostles.

CHAPTER FOUR

From the Call of the Twelve to Their Commissioning

The Twelve had been selected, but they were not sent forth to preach immediately. This motley group, however great their dedication to the Master, still needed instruction concerning the nature of their mission. Some of this information would be obtained from the Sermon on the Plain and other discourses of Jesus. Additional insight would be gained merely by being in the company of the Saviour as He walked among His people, healing those suffering from diseased bodies and ministering to those afflicted by sickness of the spirit.

1. *Sermon on the Plain, 6:20-49.* The Sermon on the Plain (6:20-49) is also referred to as the Sermon on the Mount. This obvious conclusion is drawn from a careful comparison of the two accounts. Differences are obvious, but identities and similarities are equally obvious. The only logical explanation concerning the nature of this material is that Luke chose to record in abbreviated form the larger section contained in Matthew, and at the same time elected to record some things not found in Matthew's account. Luke recorded the material which met his purpose, omitting much of particular interest to the Jew. Luke seems to have scattered much of the Matthean material throughout his gospel.

Both accounts begin with the Beatitudes. Luke recorded fewer than did Matthew, but he also recorded some "woes" which are omitted from Matthew's account. If the woes do nothing else, they do assist in emphasizing the seriousness and realism of Jesus' teachings. Both Matthew and Luke introduce the Beatitudes with the term "blessed." This term could be translated "happy," "to be congratulated spiritually," or "happy spiritually." Each beatitude is a paradox. The first recorded by Luke pertains to the poor. Jesus' world was filled with poverty, but He insisted that the poor spiritually possess a kingdom—not a kingdom of this world, but the kingdom of God.

The second beatitude speaks in terms of "blessed the ones hungering, for they shall be filled." Most of the world of Jesus' day was hungry physically, and it was unlikely that many within the world could be "filled" physically. Jesus was not speaking in terms of a physical hunger; He spoke in terms of a spiritual hunger. Those who hunger for the righteousness of God shall be filled to the point of overflowing.

Still another paradox is expressed in the words "who are weeping presently, for they shall laugh." Jesus' world was filled with weeping, but it was a weeping caused primarily by personal need. Jesus suggested that the individual who weeps over his sin is one who will know joy. A similar paradox is seen in the fourth beatitude, "Blessed are ye when men shall hate you. . . ." Jesus did not teach that men are happy spiritually whenever they are hated simply for the sake of hatred; punishment or hatred for the sake of the Son of Man brings spiritual happiness. Jesus explained (6:23) that a man can well rejoice in this day inasmuch as his treatment is not new or unique. The simple reference to the treatment of the prophets may well suggest the punishment accorded such men as Jeremiah and Isaiah.

The Beatitudes are followed by four woes (24-26). The individual who seeks happiness in material possessions has already received his consolation, his comfort. The term which is translated "have received" is a word which means "to receive full payment of an account." This word was used in the business world and was written on an account whenever the business man had received full payment. The follower of Christ will know his full payment in experience with his Lord, but the man who has a predisposition to wealth finds his only satisfaction in that possession. A similar woe is pronounced upon those who feel that they have attained full satisfaction in life; they shall know the gnawing pains of hunger. Equally sad is Jesus' teaching concerning those who believe life to be constituted of earthly and worldly pleasures; these shall mourn and weep. Jesus stated that the individual who is flattered by all men should revert to a state of abasement, because their fathers had also spoken well of false prophets. Nothing is sweeter than praise which falls upon the human ear, but praise can be short-lived.

The sermon to this point has described the citizens of God's heavenly kingdom. Certain conditions bring spiritual happiness; other spiritual conditions express themselves ultimately in spiritual sadness.

Many commentators describe 6:27 as the root of all the previous instructions. The love which Jesus describes is an unselfish love, a love which places its object at the point of highest esteem. It is the love of intelligent comprehension. His followers are to "go on loving their enemies." They are to "continue doing well to those who go on hating them." The next verse (6:28) also expresses the condition of the citizen by noting that Jesus' followers should "continue blessing" the ones who "continue cursing" them and "go on praying" in behalf of the ones who "continue using them despitefully." It is indicated in 6:29 that His followers are to "continue giving" the other cheek to the one who "continually strikes" the first cheek. The Christian is never to forbid the coat to the man who "continues taking up his cloak." The cloak was the upper and more valuable garment, while the coat was the undergarment and less valuable.

It is better for a Christian to conduct himself according to these precepts than for him to suffer the spirit of retaliation and vengeance. The illustration of love for fellow man concludes (6:30) with the suggestion that a follower of Christ is to "continue giving" to the man who "goes on asking you." The ethic of Jesus requires the spirit of the Saviour Himself, not the spirit of vested interest, selfish ungiving, and personal hatred.

The manner in which an individual is to love his enemy is further illustrated (6:31). This is Luke's statement of the Golden Rule. The Golden Rule had been spoken many times prior to Jesus' teaching, but always it was in the negative form—"What you would not have others do unto you, do not to them." In a positive manner, the Master insisted that the Christian do for others what he would have them do for him. The very manner of the Christian's treatment of others is ideally the manner in which he would prefer to be treated by others.

Jesus' discussion of love is concluded in 6:32-36. Verse 36 seems to provide the key to the interpretation of the previous verses. The Christian is to be merciful in the same manner in which the Father is merciful. Therefore, this love of intelligent comprehension will express itself toward sinners, not simply toward those who love the Christian; will manifest itself in doing the good thing toward all men, not merely toward the one who loves the Christian; will express itself in acts of kindness (lending) to all men, not simply to those who can reciprocate. This motivation of love brings a reward from God and a title, "children of the Highest." This passage concerning love is unlocked by v. 35, coupled with v. 36. God does not reveal His love toward the good alone, but He is merciful even to the evil and unthankful.

If the Christian practices love as Jesus has outlined its methodology, then he will "stop judging" (present imperative used with negative); neither will he condemn (literally, judge against one or judge down). Both of these prohibitions are followed by double negative constructions which indicate that a thing will never come to pass. The man who stops judging will not under any circumstances be judged by false criteria; nor will the one who stops condemning be condemned by the same condemnation. The Christian is not to have the habit of criticizing, nor is he always to be involved in the giving of judgment against another. This does not mean that he does not form opinions, but it does mean that he never becomes a prejudiced and censorious individual. Jesus' statements concerning judgment and condemnation are further explained in v.38. The essence of His teaching is that an individual will be measured by the same measurement he uses. The parable in vss. 39-40 is loosely connected to the preceding verses. Jesus knew that one's attitude toward judgment and condemnation would likely be that of his master. If the Christian himself lives according to the precepts of the scribes and Pharisees, he along with his blind leader will fall into the ditch. The teaching of v. 39 is further elucidated by v. 40. No disciple goes beyond his master; the master so impresses his disciple that he provides the goal for the disciple's life. The teacher must seek spiritual maturity, inasmuch as he knows a follower will not precede the leader.

Self-inspection is emphasized in vss.41-42. The Jew with his legalistic system was likely to behold the mote (speck) in the brother's eye, but fail to observe the utility pole in his own eye. Absurdity is the only adequate description of an attempt to remove a speck from the brother's eye when one has a pole in his own eye. Jesus calls such a man a "hypocrite," a term derived from the Greek stage and meaning "to act a part."

This emphasis upon wholesomeness and goodness was further illustrated by the reference to the trees. A simple maxim is that a good tree brings good fruit and a bad tree brings bad fruit. It is impossible for a good tree to produce corrupt fruit and a corrupt tree to produce good fruit. By the same simple maxim, a tree is known by the kind of fruit which it produces. The application of these verses (43-45) suggests that the man who is good inwardly produces good acts in his life, while the man who is bad internally produces corruption in outward manifestation. Verse 45 describes the heart as being the storehouse of man's life, and from his heart a good man brings forth good things; the evil man can only bring evil things because his heart is evil. These practical laws are operative in the lives of all men. The fruit of man's life corresponds to the quality of his heart.

The concluding section (vss. 46-49) defines a good heart and illustrates the means of achieving it. The content of v. 46 emphasizes that obedience to God is the only way to have a good heart and to acknowledge the lordship of Jesus. The man who does this is as a home builder who dug deep and placed the foundation on a rock. His home was soon tested by the rising flood waters and the rushing of those waters against the house. The house was not shaken because its foundation rested upon rock. Even so, obedience to the Lord's teaching establishes life upon the firm foundation capable of withstanding life's storms. But the disobedient man (v. 49) does not provide a solid foundation, taking the easy way in construction. His house is not built on a rock; when subjected to the same stress and strain testing other houses, it collapses. This collapse is immediate and the ruin is great. The man who establishes life as does a negligent home builder finds that his life collapses during the many tests which come. All of life is subjected to the same tests, varying only in degree.

2. *Miracles and Parables, 7:1-8:56.* These two chapters are constituted almost wholly by a series of miracles and parables. A parable might be described as an earthly story with a heavenly meaning. Perhaps a more exacting definition would be: a brief story told by way of analogy to illustrate some principal truth. A miracle may be defined as an event which transcends natural law and is thereby a departure from the normal operation or ordinary workings of nature.

(1) *Healing the Centurion's Servant, 7:1-10.* Following the giving of the Sermon on the Plain, Jesus returned to Capernaum, a border town between the territories of Herod Antipas and Philip, his brother. The centurion mentioned in the story was no ordinary soldier. Centurions were the backbone of the Roman military forces. Secular historians have described them as men capable of command, reliable, not foolhardy, and at the same time willing to die if necessary. It is likely that the centurion described in this account was in charge of the border guard, thus responsible to Herod Antipas. A servant of the centurion was critically ill and at the point of death. The centurion's obvious attraction to the servant made him resort to

extreme measures in an attempt to save his life. Luke indicates that this man had heard of Jesus' miracles; therefore, he commissioned some elders of the Jews to approach Jesus in behalf of his servant. The centurion himself was a Gentile, as is suggested by the commissioning of Jews to intercede for him and by Jesus' contrast of his faith with that of Israel (7:3,9). His wholesome relationship to the Jews is suggested by the elders' words, "He was worthy for whom he should do this: for he loveth our nation, and he hath built us a synagogue."

A man of authority, the centurion realized the value and effectiveness of authority and submission. Thus, upon learning that Jesus was not far from his house, he sent friends to insist that Jesus should not be troubled to come there. The Master should not be annoyed by this needless trip; a word from the Master would suffice. As a commander of troops, he had witnessed many times the effectiveness of a command, and he was sure that Jesus' command for the healing of his servant would be equally effective. Jesus used this friend's faith as a challenge to the Jew, noting that He had not found this kind of faith among the Jews.

(2) *Raising the Widow's Son, 7:11-18.* The previous miracle indicates the ability of Jesus to heal a critically ill man although removed geographically. The miracle recorded in this section reveals that this power is effective not only for the diseased body, but also for the lifeless body. Nain was south of Capernaum and was located against the slopes of Little Hermon. The tragedy of death was intensified by the fact that this widow had lost her only son. She was accompanied by the usual group of mourners as the procession moved from the gate of the city to the burial site. In all probability, the mother walked in front of the funeral bier and was accompanied by friends, curiosity seekers, and the customary hired mourners who carried their flutes and cymbals.

Jesus approached the group and commanded the mother to "stop weeping." He then touched the funeral bier and spoke directly to the young man. The fact is significant that He said, "I say to you, be raised." He did not identify the *I*. The Master of life and death in a cruel world had come to the assistance of a widowed mother who depended entirely upon her only son. The dead boy sat up and began to speak. All the people feared and "continued to glorify" God because of the Saviour's power. They proclaimed that "a great prophet is risen and God hath visited his people." This work of Jesus was reported throughout all Judea and the surrounding regions.

This particular miracle is incisive and significant because it indicates the Saviour's power over death as well as over disease. It is also significant that for the first time in his gospel Luke refers to Jesus as "Lord." This term was to become the favorite term used by Jesus' followers. He became their Master of life in the same sense in which the slave was subjected to his master.

(3) *Approval of John's Ministry, 7:19-35.* John the Baptist had been imprisoned because of his stern denunciation of Herod Antipas' adulterous relationship with Herodias. While he was imprisoned, his disciples reported to him. As a forerunner, he had expected quick and complete victory for the Messiah; but from Herod's prison the future seemed to be growing darker and darker. His inquiry is quite logical and understandable. Was this actually the Messiah? Had he been mistaken? Should he look for another yet to come? A report of many miracles constituted Jesus' answer. "Tell John that the infirm are made whole, the evil spirits are exorcised, the blind see, the lepers are cleansed, the deaf hear, the dead are raised, and the gospel is preached to the poor." He warned John that the man who is not offended in Christ is blessed. Jesus further warned John not to be misled by his own mistaken ideas or his own discouragement in prison. The claim of Jesus in 7:23 is firm and authoritative.

The departure of John's messengers provided Jesus with the opportunity to speak a word of genuine appreciation for John. He reminds His hearers that John's ministry was set in the wilderness background; and yet crowds went to the wilderness to hear him, not to see a blade of grass being blown by the wind. Neither had they been attracted to a man in appealing attire; rather, they had been attracted by a prophet, a preparer, a forerunner of the Messiah. Jesus (7:27) indicates that John's work was a fulfillment of prophecy. Because he is a prophet and the immediate forerunner of the Lord, he is the greatest of all prophets. He actually saw the Messiah, publicly introduced Him, and continued to proclaim the Messiah's message. Yet, the least in the kingdom is greater than John, the forerunner. His place was one of preparation. This is not to eliminate John from the blessings provided by Jesus, but rather establishes his work as belonging to the preparatory stage. The most insignificant citizen of the kingdom is superior to John.

Luke (7:31-35) describes in the simplest terms the generation in which John and Jesus lived. In one moment they were as children who wished to "play funeral," and in another moment they were as children who wished to "play marriage." John was an ascetic, but they rejected him. Jesus identified Himself with His generation but was also rejected, being described as a winebibber and friend of sinners. But wisdom is recognized by all related to her. God's follower recognizes the work of God in John's ministry and also sees the work of the Father in the ministry of His Son. God placed His stamp of approval upon the action of Jesus. For 30 years He had lived as a perfect Man. Now the perfect Son had identified Himself totally and completely with His eternal mission. Fully identified as the eternal Son and perfectly accepted as God's beloved Son, Jesus was ready to begin the long journey culminating in victory over sin.

(4) *Parable of the Debtor and Related Teachings, 7:36-50.* Simon, a legalistic Pharisee, invited Jesus to a meal in his house. As any good Pharisee, he would be recognized for his legalism and his professed religion. He serves well as a personal illustration of the words immediately preceding in which Jesus describes His generation as "children . . . in the market place . . . calling to one another. . . ." The other primary character in this account is a woman described as a sinner. Judging from the scant information given, it seems as if she were simply a "woman of the street." However, she ministered to Jesus in a way that the Pharisee did not. She expressed her love by standing at Jesus' feet, washing His dusty feet with her tears, and then wiping them with her hair. She kissed His feet and anointed them. Here in Capernaum as elsewhere, the Jewish women valued ointment as one of their most cherished possessions. Is there a possible suggestion in the conviction that her most precious possession was suitable enough only for the Master's feet?

Simon's observation (7:39) reveals his true evaluation of Jesus' character. His statement could be translated in this way: "This man, if he were a prophet—which he is not—would have known who and what manner of woman this is—which he does not." Simon's simple conclusion is that Jesus is a sinner. Jesus responds with the parable of the debtors. One man owed 500 pence to his creditor, the other only one-tenth as much. Neither was able to pay his account, but the creditor forgave both. Jesus then inquired which of these men would have loved the creditor more. Simon replied that the one to whom more had been forgiven would have had more love for the creditor. Jesus agreed and used the parable and Simon's answer as a springboard from which to address His accuser. He reminded Simon that as host he had not even offered to wash the Master's feet, a responsibility usually relegated to the lowest slave in the household. Nor did

Simon honor Jesus with a kiss, although the woman incessantly kissed the Master's feet.

Jesus then states the basic teaching—the greater the forgiveness, the greater the love. Jesus straightforwardly declared that the woman's sins were forgiven, His last remark being, "Go in peace."

(5) *Parable of the Sower, 8:1-15*. Luke's transition from the parable of the debtors to the parable of the sower is marked by a brief teaching concerning the devout women who ministered to His needs. Luke describes Jesus' ministry as one of constant activity. He seemed to contact every town and village, continually preaching and manifesting the glad tidings of the kingdom. On these journeys He was accompanied by the Twelve, and obviously their needs were great. These women "were ministering" (imperfect tense, describing continuous action in past time) to Jesus' group from their substance. The verb suggests that they were ministering to Him as the table waiter assists the diners. Only three of the women are identified. Mary Magdalene, from whom Jesus had cast seven devils, is numbered among them. One who was possessed of seven devils had a special infestation. The Jews attached great significance to the number seven; this can be readily seen from Matthew 12:45. Joanna, whose husband was Chuza, a steward of Herod, also ministered to him. Chuza was a man of authority and respect, caring for the personal properties of Herod. Susanna is the third identified by name. She is not mentioned elsewhere in the New Testament, and scholars are reluctant even to conjecture concerning her background and identity. This brief notation by Luke concerning the women who ministered to Jesus and the apostles indicates that Jesus continually refused to use His power for selfish interests.

The parables of Jesus present extensive lessons. The term "parable" means literally "to place alongside, to cast alongside." Jesus did not employ parabolic material which was confusing to His followers; rather, He chose the common things to illustrate spiritual truths.

The parable of the sower pictures the Jewish farmer in the process of sowing grain. His only equipment was a grain bag and a strong arm with which to cast the seeds. With such "unmechanical equipment" as this, some seed would be wasted while other seed would fall on fertile soil. Although the parable is generally referred to as the parable of the sower, it could better be referred to as the parable of the soils. The emphasis is not upon the sower; it is upon the different kinds of soils. Some of the seed fell by the path serving as a dividing line between various fields. These seed were trampled, gained no rootage, and birds devoured them. Other seed fell upon rocky soil which gave immediate rootage. However, these plants soon withered because rocky soil has no depth quality. Other seed fell on ground filled with thorns, but it appeared clean at the moment. The weed seeds and wild grass roots which remained grew with the grain and eventually choked the grain plants. Still other seed fell on good fertile ground, germinated, and bore fruit a hundredfold. After briefly stating the parable, Jesus terminates the account with the succinct statement, "He that hath ears to hear, let him hear." The man who is prepared spiritually to interpret spiritual truth should hear the teaching of Jesus.

Jesus explains (v. 10) that God had given the disciples the ability to know the mysteries (deeper truths) concerning the kingdom; to the ears of Jesus' followers, deeper truths were involved in the simple words of the seed and soils. However, these words merely related the routine story of a Jewish farmer to the ears of the unenlightened. Jesus further explains that the very privilege of hearing becomes a curse and punishment to the multitudes. They have seen His works, but they *did not truly see*; they have heard, but they *did not comprehend*. Jesus' ministry must now be restricted to those who wished to understand. On many previous occasions He had taught the multitudes, but they had seemed to be attracted only by His ability to meet physical needs. Now He employs the parable to make truth simple and plain. The spiritual truth that was simple and plain to the one who followed Jesus was equally confused and disguised to the unbeliever.

The explanation of the parable is as brief and concise as the parable. The seed is God's Word; the one who removes the Word is the devil; the seeds falling on the rocky soil are emotional hearers; the seeds falling among thorns represent God's words being choked by the cares and riches of the world; the seeds falling on good ground are the followers who bear fruit in His kingdom. Thus the parable could rightly be identified as the parable of the soils.

(6) *Parable of the Lamp, 8:16-18.* The brief parable of the lamp further illustrates the purpose and responsibility of discipleship. A lamp exists for the purpose of producing light. It is not lighted and then covered, nor is it placed under a bed. A lamp is placed on a candlestick that those entering the house may "go on seeing" the light. A purpose clause expresses the conception that a light is to illuminate. With these words the Lord dispels the thought that He speaks so as not to be understood. He does speak in parables in order

to be more easily understood, but the sensitivity of the hearer deter-
mines the value of the parable. Here, as elsewhere in the New
Testament, nothing is known of a secret faith. Faith radiates and
manifests itself. Verse 18 indicates the importance and significance of
hearing. The Christian would do well to forget some things, but other
things should be heard and treasured. The hearer who possesses the
truth will possess even more; the hearer who refuses to hear may even
lose the privilege of hearing.

(7) *A Definition of Spiritual Relationship, 8:19-21.* The account of a visit paid Jesus by His mother and brothers follows
immediately in Luke's record. They found Him surrounded by a
multitude and were therefore unable to get near Him. Having been
told that His mother and brothers desired to see Him, Jesus replied:
"My mother and my brethren are those which hear the word of God,
and do it." To be "related" to Jesus is to do His will. Obedience is a
basic sign of spiritual relationship. The event is also recorded in
Matthew 12:48 and Mark 3:31. From these two accounts, one understands that Jesus' relatives believed Him to be exerting Himself and
desired that He return home with them.

(8) *Stilling the Sea, 8:22-25.* The Marcan parallel (4:35ff.)
discloses the occasion for Jesus' suggestion that the group journey to
the other side of the lake. The request came at the end of a long and
busy day. Jesus had been engaged in extensive teaching, employing
the parabolic method. Tired and exhausted, He suggested that the
group travel to an isolated place. This beautiful body of water could
suddenly be marred by a vicious storm. Such a storm occurred during
this journey.

It must be assumed that these skilled fishermen used every
"trick of the trade" in an attempt to negotiate the waters and avoid
waking the Master. However, their boat "was filling" with water and
they were in danger. The only avenue remaining to them was to enlist
the Master's assistance; they cried, "Master, Master, we perish." The
verb (present tense) suggests they were in the process of perishing.
Jesus arose and in His unassuming manner calmed the waves, again
demonstrating His power over nature. Jesus investigated the reason
for their fear by asking, "Where is your faith?" The Lord of history
and the Lord of nature was present in the ship. Why should they
fear? The disciples' only response was in their continued questioning
of one another, "What manner of man is this? . . . He commands

even the winds and the water and they obey him." Jesus' point had been well made.

(9) *Healing the Gadarene Demoniac, 8:26-40.* Jesus and His disciples soon arrived in the country of the Gadarenes. The point of departure had been Capernaum and the destination was Gergesa. The demoniac, who abode in the tombs, met Jesus. He had been demon-possessed for an extended period and wore no clothing. Yet, as soon as he came to Jesus, he fell before Him and cried, "What to me and to you, Jesus, Son of the Most High God? I beg you, do not ever begin to torment me." Luke explains the demon's requests by indicating that Jesus commanded the unclean spirit to depart. The extreme physical condition was brought by the demoniac powers (8:29). To bind the poor man with chains and fetters was an impossibility.

Jesus then addressed the man with the question, "What is thy name?" The man replied, "Legion." The shackled man realized that he was possessed by many demons, which then began begging Jesus that He not send them back into the abyss, the present abode of demons. Their very nature caused them to desire to infest some man or animal; and inasmuch as a herd of hogs fed on the mountain, they exhorted Jesus to send them into the swine. Jesus answered their request, and the infested swine ran violently into the sea. The action of the swine was clearly unnatural. The keepers of the swine then fled to the city and related the details of the swine's drownings and the demoniac's healing. Curiosity seekers quickly came to the wilderness area and found the demoniac clothed, mentally stable, and tranquil at the feet of Jesus.

This miracle has occasioned much criticism of the Saviour. Some commentators have indicated that He had no right to destroy personal property. Others have suggested simply that the man's cries and screams disturbed the swine and caused them to dash into the sea. Regardless of one's interpretation of the event, it must be remembered that Jesus valued the demoniac more highly than He did the swine. The important thing is that a man who described himself as Legion (a Roman legion contained some 6,000 men) was freed from the demons and resumed a normal life.

This miracle produced different results on various groups. The Gadarenes came to Jesus and asked Him to leave their country. The demoniac, on the contrary, desired to remain with Jesus, but Jesus sent him away, commanding him to go into his own house and there reveal what God had done for him. A sad note falls on the joyous scene when Luke declares that Jesus never returned to the land of the Gadarenes.

(10) *Raising Jairus' Daughter, 8:41-56.* A mass of people waited for the Lord and among them was Jairus. As ruler of the synagogue, Jairus was responsible for the administration of the synagogue affairs and the planning of synagogue worship. His post was one of highest respect and suggested that he had climbed the ladder of success. Yet, all his success and respect were forgotten when he came to Jesus, fell at Jesus' feet, and revealed that his daughter was dying. The pathos of the moment is further defined by Luke's description of the girl, who was only 12 years of age. A great multitude of people thronged Jesus as He honored Jairus' request and began the journey to His house.

Included in the multitude was a woman who for 12 years had suffered from an incurable physical condition. Luke states that she had spent all her money for medical assistance but had not been cured. She pushed through the crowds and eventually came near enough to touch the border of Jesus' garment, possibly a tassel of the over garment. She was immediately healed. Jesus knew that power had gone from His body and asked, "Who touched me?" Peter reminded Him that a great multitude had crowded about Him. Why should He ask, "Who touched me?" Jesus explained His question on the basis of an awareness of virtue passing from His body.

Jesus' omniscience manifested itself in His recognition of her touch and the awareness of the departure of healing power from His body. It is significant to understand that healing cost Jesus something. He did not work as a magician, but rather as a miracle worker. Realizing that she could not be disguised before the eyes of the Master, the woman came, fell at His feet, explained her reason for touching Him, and declared her wholeness. Jesus then commended her faith, explaining that the healing was due to faith, not merely to the touching of His garment. She had come a disturbed individual, knowing only a wretched existence. Now she left clean, pure, unblighted by disease, and with a quality of peace which mere physical recovery could never bring.

While Jesus was speaking to the woman, a messenger came from Jairus' house and suggested that Jairus not trouble the Master inasmuch as the girl had already died. Jesus then entered the conversation by speaking words which had become so prominent in Luke's gospel, "Stop fearing." If Jairus would believe, his daughter would be made whole. When Jesus and His group arrived at Jairus' home, He took the inner circle of disciples (Peter, James, and John), and the girl's parents into the room where her body lay. All were weeping and expressing their sorrow, but Jesus commanded them to "Stop weeping." He suggested that she was only asleep, but this suggestion brought mere ridicule. To notice that Jesus used a term ordinary to life in referring to the sad experience of death is important. As one awakes to sleep and sleeps to awake, even so one lives to die and dies to live. His miraculous power would soon awaken the maiden. He took her by the hand and commanded her to arise. The girl immediately arose and ate meat. The eating of meat indicated the completeness of her restoration and a return to normalcy. Astonishment characterized the parents, who were told to remain silent concerning this event. But how could the parents remain silent following her restoration to life?

For Further Study

1. Study John Broadus' discussion of the similarities and differences between the Sermon on the Mount and the Sermon on the Plain, "Matthew," *An American Commentary on the New Testament*, pp. 83-86.
2. Define the term "beatitude." Contrast the terms "beatitude" and "woe."
3. Read a discussion of the term "miracle" in one of the following:
   The Interpreter's Dictionary of the Bible, pp. 392-402.
   The New Smith's Bible Dictionary, p. 243.
   The Zondervan Pictorial Bible Dictionary, pp. 544-546.
4. Define the term "resurrection." Contrast the raising of Jairus' daughter and the resurrection of Jesus.
5. Define a centurion. Compare his position with that of a contemporary army officer.

CHAPTER FIVE

The Commissioning and Training
of the Twelve

During an extended period of time, Jesus had observed His followers and had evaluated their potentialities. The scope of His ministry had continued to enlarge; the time for commissioning His apostles had arrived. To this point Jesus had not directed His apostles into independent ministries, but had chosen to instruct the group as they accompanied Him.

1. *Commissioning of the Twelve, 9:1-6.* To this point the apostles had simply been companions of Jesus and had engaged in little work independent of His presence and leadership. At this time, Jesus called the Twelve, gave them directions for their work, and provided instructions concerning their provisions and personal decorum. These instructions were not given for their future ministries; the Lord instructed them concerning this assigned mission.

The miraculous power which Jesus gave to the apostles was to be used in exorcising demons and curing diseased bodies. This ability of Jesus immediately removed Him from the category of an ordinary human leader. Regardless of man's ability to lead and to guide, he never possesses the ability to transfer this gift to someone else. Their ministry was to be a ministry of mercy and preaching. Their responsibility was to proclaim the kingdom of God and to heal the sick. The significance and importance of their responsibility is seen in His exhortation that they take no provisions with them; they were to depend upon God. Their time was not to be consumed by moving from house to house, but they were to remain in one location until they departed from that city. If they were not received, upon departing from the city they were to shake the dust from their feet. The act indicated the breaking of all relationships, and by shaking the specks of dust from their clothing the disciples suggested complete withdrawal. This was customarily practiced by the Jew upon returning to Palestine from a Gentile country. Stopping at the border of Palestine, the Jew shook the dust of the pagan lands from his sandals. Luke's brief discussion of the apostles' ministry is amplified by comparing the parallel passages in Matthew 10:1 ff., and Mark 3:13 ff.

2. *Herod and John the Baptist, 9:7-9.* When Herod Antipas heard of the apostles' ministries, he was thoroughly at a loss to find any explanation for their works. Added to his personal difficulty was the report of some that John the Baptizer had been raised from the dead. Herod had earlier executed John because of the forerunner's accusations against the tetrarch and Herodias, his brother's wife. Some of the Jews identified the works of the Twelve with Elijah; others simply indicated that a dead prophet had been raised. Attempting to reassure himself, Herod insisted that John had been beheaded. But this did not resolve the difficulty. The question remained: "Who is this of whom such things are spoken?" Other gospel accounts disclose that Herod's guilty conscience created fear, lest the executed forerunner had been raised from the dead.

3. *Special Training of the Disciples, 9:10-56.* The major portion of Luke 9 describes briefly Jesus' training of the Twelve. Some of these events are described more completely in other accounts: Luke proposes to record the essentials relating to this period of training.

(1) *Provisions for the Five Thousand, 9:10-17.* The excited disciples returned with glowing accounts of victory. The term "declared" is a word meaning "to relate a narrative through to the end." In all probability the apostles returned to Capernaum, the city which Jesus had adopted as the headquarters for His Galilean ministry. Jesus, however, led the disciples from the multitudes to a desert place belonging to the city called Bethsaida. Mark (6:31) explains that one reason for Jesus' leading His disciples into the desert was to permit them to rest. Yet, the people heard of their journey and followed them. The compassionate Saviour did not refuse the multitudes, but spent the day in preaching the kingdom of God and in healing those who were ill.

Toward the end of the day, the Twelve asked Jesus to send the multitudes away that they might secure food in the surrounding villages. But Jesus had other ideas and commanded the apostles to feed the multitudes. Five thousand men would require more than five loaves and two fishes! Jesus' reaction is a study of order and uniformity. Having commanded that the men be divided into companies of 50, He then took the available food, looked to heaven, blessed the food, and broke it. It then became the responsibility of the disciples to distribute the food. Jesus never used His miraculous power in a selfish manner, but in this instance it is obvious that He used His power to provide physical necessities. The scripture indicates that they ate and were filled. Yet, none of the food was wasted. The disciples filled 12 baskets with fragments. Jesus' provisions exceeded the needs of 5,000 men.

This is the only miracle recorded in each of the gospels (cf. Matthew 14:15 ff.; Mark 6:30 ff.; John 6:1 ff.). These beautiful words show the Saviour's divine power. This miracle may assume special meaning when one remembers that the Jews often conceived of the Messiah's coming as pictured in a messianic banquet. Jesus often used such terms. For example, He spoke of being seated at the table in the kingdom of God (Luke 13:29), of the great banquet (14:15-24), and of meeting the needs of the poor (4:18). Perhaps this miracle depicts the festivities of the Messianic Age. The Messiah had fed them even as He would continue to nourish them spiritually.

(2) *The Great Confession, 9:18-22.* Luke departs from the Marcan framework at this point, omitting the events related in Mark 6:45-8:26. That the author is not attempting a full biography of Jesus is obvious. Just as John selected signs relevant to his purpose (John 20:30-31), Luke recorded materials essential to presenting Jesus as the Universal Saviour.

Luke again mentions the prayer life of the Saviour. In such an experience, He asked His disciples, "Who say the people that I am?" As stated previously (9:7-9), some suggested Jesus was John the Baptist, others identified Him as Elijah, while still others believed Him to be one of the old prophets who had been raised from death. The opinions concerning His identity varied, but Jesus was more interested in the opinion of His followers than in the opinions of the multitudes. Peter chose to answer the question and did so in a straightforward and blunt manner: "The Christ of God." Much of the detail which is recorded in Matthew (16:13-20) is omitted by Luke. Jesus commanded the disciples not to share this information, insisting that the Son of Man must suffer, be slain, and be resurrected. No Jew thought of the Messiah as a suffering servant. Rather, He was depicted as a military deliverer, a prophet, a priest, even a king—but not a suffering servant.

Perhaps Jesus imposed silence upon His disciples because they were not prepared to interpret His Messiahship. Although He had declared Himself to be the Messiah by indicating that the miracles of the Messianic Age had been fulfilled in His ministry (7:22), He was on the threshold of beginning a massive educational program in which He would seek to alter the Jewish conceptions possessed by the disciples and to instill in them an appreciation and understanding of the true nature of the Messianic kingdom. It is true that the Twelve had seen more in Jesus than the multitudes had observed. Yet, it is also true that their understanding of Messiahship, death, and resurrection was only embryonic in nature.

(3) *Principles of Discipleship, 9:23-27.* If Jesus' word concerning Messiahship was shocking and revolutionary, much more were His words concerning the discipline of His followers. Jesus points out that a man chooses to become His follower. Discipleship is not something thrust upon a man, but something chosen by the man after weighing the evidences and counting the costs. However, once he has chosen to follow Jesus, he denies ("says no decisively to himself") and decisively bears his cross daily. Jesus further explains (9:24) the merits of discipleship by indicating that the man who is willing to lose his life for the sake of the Gospel shall save it. Spiritual suicide is committed by the individual who clings desperately to his life, thereby attempting to save it. In contemporary parlance, a man may gain all the wealth in the world—including that of the oil companies, banks, insurance companies, brokerage firms, realtors, etc.—but if he loses his soul, he has driven a poor bargain. Jesus' suffering (v. 26) ultimately reveals His glory. The individual who blushes because of a suffering Christ should be aware that Christ will be glorified on that day with the glory of God and the holy angels. This glory is a part of His retinue in the day of His return.

Verse 27 has been interpreted variously. The words "till they see the kingdom of God" may refer to the transfiguration, the resurrection, the destruction of Jerusalem, or to the parousia of the Lord. It must be remembered that Jesus said, "Some standing here will not taste of death till they see the kingdom of God." This obviously means that some of His hearers will not die before they see the kingdom of God come. He refers to some special event. It seems likely that this event was the destruction of Jerusalem inasmuch as it was decisive, known by all, and made possible the recognition and appreciation of Christianity in a way impossible prior to the destruction of the city and its temple. When Jerusalem was destroyed, God revealed that the old ceremonial dispensation had ceased and that the new dispensation had truly been initiated.

(4) *Transfiguration of Jesus, 9:28-36.* The transfiguration account is also recorded in Matthew (17:1 ff.) and Mark (9:10 ff.). Again, Jesus looked to the inner circle for strength. To them the greater revelation of His person was to be given. Peter, James, and John accompanied Jesus to a mountain (perhaps Hermon) to pray. While He was praying, "the form of his face (became) another and his countenance white flashing forth." No conjunction appears between the terms "white" and "glistering" (flashing forth). Unique to the phenomenon was the appearance of two men—Moses and Elijah —who were speaking. These men appeared in their heavenly glory and were discussing His exodus to be accomplished in Jerusalem. The disciples were fatigued and slept for some time but were suddenly awakened and saw His glory. But another equally strange phenomenon was added to the scene. The six entered into a cloud which was overshadowing them. Luke seems to indicate (v. 34) that only the disciples feared. Their fear was unfounded, for a voice came from the cloud saying, "This is my beloved Son; hear him." Once the voice was silenced, the disciples and Jesus were left alone. Elijah and Moses had disappeared, as had the cloud and voice. Peter then said, "Master, it is good thus to be here: let us make three booths—one for you and one for Moses and one for Elijah." The Matthean account reminds the reader that Jesus pledged the disciples to silence, while Luke simply records that they told no one of these things.

The transfiguration of the Lord is denied by some interpreters who simply explain away the experience. According to this approach, the transfiguration could be explained merely as a symbolic story but one without any historical substance. Still other interpreters have sought to explain it upon the basis of natural factors—floating morning clouds and hazy sunlight, plus the half-conscious state which exists between alertness and sleep. The only logical explanation is a third, and this one accepts the gospel account in its entirety. This however, is not to suggest that anyone fully comprehends the experience. Jesus' transfiguration is important to the Christian because of the revelation of His divine majesty and eternal glory (9:20-31). Furthermore, it is important because of the subject discussed by Jesus, Moses, and Elijah. The three discussed His approaching exodus, His death in Jerusalem. Moreover, the heavenly voice declared Jesus to be the final authority in religious experience. Moses represented the law and all of its significance, and Elijah served as a representative of the prophetic ministry. However, it was not to the law or the prophets that the voice referred, but to the Son of God, the final authority in religious experience.

(5) *Healing the Demoniac Boy, 9:37-45.* After leaving the mountain, Jesus and His disciples journeyed into the valley where many people met them. A particular father began to beg Jesus to heal his demoniac son. The lad cried violently, great drops of saliva fell from his mouth, and the spirit bruised him, leaving the lad few moments of peace. Added to the seriousness of the hour is the fact that Jesus' disciples had been unable to cast out the demon. They previously had enjoyed divine power in exorcising demons, but this power had not been maintained.

The first words spoken by Jesus were addressed to the faithless disciples. He then requested that the son be brought to Him. Jesus rebuked the devil, healed the child, and returned the boy to his father. These actions created amazement at the grandeur and evident manifestation of God's power. While the multitudes were marveling at Jesus' actions, He said, "You yourselves put into your ears these words: for the Son of Man is about to be given over into hands of men." Yet, the disciples did not comprehend these words. Luke explains that the meaning was hidden from them. Later they would remember these words and realize that Jesus had met His agony and suffering with full knowledge and comprehension of these future events. But at this time, they did not have the courage to request an explanation. The suggestion that their Messiah would suffer and die was incomprehensible.

(6) *Teaching Concerning True Greatness, 9:46-50.* The remotest suggestion of an earthly kingdom seems always to have triggered some dispute among the disciples, who at this time argued among themselves concerning which one should be greatest in this kingdom. This was no academic question or theoretical discussion but related directly to a personal problem existing within the group. Jesus illustrated true greatness by placing a child by His side and then suggesting that the one who received the child received the Saviour. By the same token, the one who received the Saviour received the One who sent the Saviour. The child could not assist anyone, nor was he able to bring greatness or honor to any man. But Jesus said that the greatest among the disciples would be the least. It is this spirit that makes possible the receiving of the Saviour. One must learn to be small before he can become great!

This teaching occasioned an expression of intolerance on the part of John. The disciples had observed a man who exorcised devils in Jesus' name, but they had reprimanded this servant because he did not follow the apostolic band. The prohibition of Jesus could best be translated, "Stop hindering him." Jesus further explains the error of their decision by indicating that whoever is not against you is "in behalf of you." The man reprimanded by the disciples was a humble man who had a faith in Jesus which effected the exorcising of demons. Therefore, their attitudes were in error in two points: (1) They misunderstood the nature and source of the man's power. (2) They misunderstood the servant's purpose.

(7) *His Purpose in Life, 9:51-56.* Luke employs a common Greek idiom to indicate that the time for Jesus' ministry in Jerusalem had come. All was in readiness for Jesus' passion. The forerunner had long since completed his task. Jesus had repeatedly revealed Himself to the multitudes. The Saviour had patiently and meticulously instructed His followers. With the same decisiveness revealed in closing the door to the carpenter's shop and leaving the city of Nazareth to identify Himself with the movement of John the Baptist, He determined that this was the time to journey to Jerusalem. The use (9:51) of *autos,* a personal pronoun used intensively, intensifies this idea. *He Himself,* possessed by a crystallization of purpose, determined to go to Jerusalem, the center of Judaism and Jewish worship. To go there was to endanger His life. To refuse to go was to disobey God's purpose.

In two additional verses (13:22; 17:11) Luke mentions Jesus' journey toward the city. That Jesus traveled through Samaria is worthy of note. The Samaritans were hated by the Jews because of their intermarriage with their Syrian captors. Jesus determined to travel by Mount Gerizim, the site of the Samaritan Temple, and by so doing further repudiated it. Although messengers preceded Jesus, the Samaritans refused to accept Him because He purposed to go to Jerusalem. As would be expected in the heart of a Jew, this rejection created a great problem for James and John and for others of the disciples. These two asked if they should call fire from heaven to consume them as Elijah had done to consume the prophets of Baal. But Jesus rebuked them, explaining this rebuke on the lack of understanding, both of the disciples' relationship to the Saviour and of the Saviour's basic purposes. James and John, the "sons of thunder," were zealous for their Master and His honor, but they failed to remember that Jesus had come to save men, not to destroy them. Therefore, Jesus and His band simply left this village and traveled to another.

FOR FURTHER STUDY

1. Read Stewart Perowne's *The Later Herods*, pp. 18-27, 41-56, for a discussion of Herod Antipas.

2. What is the importance of the Great Confession to the ministry of Jesus? To the testimony of the apostles? See A. M. Hunter's *The Gospel According to Mark*, pp. 91-93.

3. Compare the transfiguration account (9:28-36) and Paul's account of Christ's self-emptying (Philippians 2:1-11).

4. Contrast, by defining the similarities and differences, true greatness as defined by Jesus and our world.

5. Study carefully Luke 9:50-56, the section describing Jesus' purpose in life. Should the Christian have an equally definite purpose? How does your purpose differ from His?

Part III

The Saviour Journeys to Jerusalem

CHAPTER SIX

Initial Stages of the Journey

The account to this point has provided an insight into the parables, miracles, and the general teaching ministry of the Saviour. Numerous events indicative of Jesus' power over nature and death have been recorded. The simplicity of His teaching has been emphasized by His parabolic method. The stage is now set for the disclosure of Jesus' deliberate intent to minister in Jerusalem. This extensive section, 9:57-19:28, relates events which occurred while Jesus traveled toward the Holy City.

1. *His Servants, 9:57-10:24.* These brief verses constitute an insight into the attitudes of Jesus' followers. Some were indifferent to the point of being undisciplined; others were excited to the point of rejoicing in the Lord's power.

(1) *Half-hearted Followers, 9:57-62.* Jesus' ministry always offered love, yet it also offered a challenge. Luke identifies a certain man, called a scribe (Matthew 8:19), who came to Jesus and asserted his loyalty by insisting that he would follow wherever Jesus traveled. Jesus reminded him that foxes have dens, birds have nests to call their own, but the Son of Man has no place to call His home. Following Him does not result in materialistic wealth. Neither does discipleship result in a place of materialistic honor and superiority. The man did not comprehend the sacrifice involved in this discipleship.

On a second occasion, Jesus commanded a man to follow him. This man explained his willingness to become a disciple, but first he must minister the burial rites to his father. This responsibility

(Genesis 25:9) was considered a sacred duty, but it would seem as if this man's father were still alive. He obviously suggested to Jesus that he could not become His follower until first he had buried his father. To this, Jesus replied that the dead are to bury their dead. The most obvious explanation is that the spiritual dead can bury the physical dead. This response may seem harsh, but it must be remembered that the prospective disciple was using an aged father as an excuse for his failure to respond to Jesus' call.

Another volunteered to follow the Lord, but requested that he have the privilege of saying good-by to those in his home. But Jesus cannot accept any excuse and requires that the man become His follower and devoted disciple; He cannot accept half-hearted dedication and service. His statement is a forceful pronouncement concerning indifference toward service. If a man puts his hand to the plow and looks backward, he plows a crooked and uneven furrow. This is not fit performance for a qualified farmer, nor is it acceptable to a Saviour who requires whole-heartedness in service.

Luke does not give further insight into the characters or the futures of these three men, but the words of the Saviour leave a solemn injunction to all His followers. Half-heartedness has no place in the kingdom of God!

(2) *Commissioning the Seventy, 10:1-16.* The mission of the Seventy must be interpreted in the light of "the time was come that he should be received . . ." (9:51). Apart from this consideration, the urgency of the Seventy's mission is misinterpreted. On another occasion, he had sent the Twelve (cf. 9:1-10). Instructions given to the Seventy were similar to those given to the Twelve. The Seventy were sent in pairs to places that Jesus Himself purposed to visit. It would seem as if their work were something similar to that of John, the forerunner. In the Trans-Jordan area, to which these were sent, the spiritual need was indeed great, the number of laborers few. The term "harvest" would immediately strike a responsive chord in the heart of any Jew. Whenever the grain was ripe and ready for threshing, it had to be threshed immediately lest the next year's food supply be lost. In this analogy, Jesus illustrated the emergency existing in the drought-stricken hearts of many.

The task assigned the Seventy was described as difficult, their being much as lambs in the midst of wolves (10:3). They were not to carry their provisions, nor were they to spend their time idly in greeting men met on the highway (10:4). Whenever they entered a house, they were to employ the typical Jewish greeting, "Peace be to this house." If the owner of the house accepted the message of the kingdom, then the "Son of peace" was there and the disciples' peace would rest upon the house. If these conditions did not exist, then the blessing would return to the individual who gave it.

Jesus prohibited the disciples' moving from house to house while in the same village, insisting that they were to remain in the same house and partake of the hospitality offered by their host. Jesus also reminded the disciples that a "laborer is worthy of his hire" (10:7). The fact that Gentiles lived in the Trans-Jordan area is evident by the admonition to "eat such things as are set before you" (10:8). Their mission was one of healing as well as one of preaching (10:9). And yet, the mercy of healing was related directly to the presence of the kingdom.

The last section of Jesus' instructions (10:16) contains some fearful warnings. Whenever a city refused to accept two of the emissaries, the men were to shake the dust of the city from their feet and clothing; but this enactment was to be interpreted with the announcement of the kingdom's nearness. The seriousness of rejecting the messengers sent by Jesus is further described in the analogy drawn between the rejecters and the ancient city of Sodom. The people of Chorazin and Bethsaida had already voiced their rejection of Jesus. The inhabitants of these cities had ample opportunity to know and appreciate the works of the Saviour. Jesus reveals that Tyre and Sidon would have long since repented had they as much revelation as Chorazin and Bethsaida. Their repentance would have been characterized by sackcloth and ashes, meaningful characteristics of sorrow and repentance. Jesus further indicated that it would be more tolerable in the hour of judgment for Tyre and Sidon than for Chorazin and Bethsaida, cities which had received greater revelation.

Capernaum, the headquarters for Jesus' Galilean ministry, had exalted itself but had nevertheless rejected the revelation which Jesus had provided. Jesus stated that these peoples would be cast down to Hades. This term suggests the total desolation which Jesus prophesied would come upon the area.

(3) *The Seventy's Report, 10:17-24.* In all probability Jesus designated the site where He would meet the returning disciples. Their first statement upon reunion with Jesus concerned the realization of divine power in the exorcising of demons. Although the disciples were without explanation for the demons' submission, Jesus explained it on the basis of Satan's power having been broken. The breaking of the devil's power began with Jesus' temptation and

continued throughout His ministry to Gethsemane, and beyond to the cross. The expression, "beheld Satan as lightning fall from heaven," interprets the completeness of Satan's shackling. As the lightning flashes across the darkened sky and suddenly vanishes, in similar fashion Satan falls. The completeness of Jesus' power is further revealed by the strong statement concerning His protection of His people. Although the disciples may have taken this as an occasion for rejoicing, Jesus carefully reminded them that the gift of power was not the primary occasion for rejoicing; rather, it was the promise of a heavenly home. Surely the disciples would understand that the One who gave them the power to conquer their severest enemies was capable of writing their names in the heavenly record.

That Jesus turned to thank the Father for His revelation to the simplest person is reason for additional emphasis upon this experience. Jesus' prayer of thanksgiving suggests again that God chose to reveal Himself to the simplest person, not to the wise and prudent (scribes). God's revelation is centered in Christ (10:22). This verse remarkably reviews the Son's relationship to the Father. Jesus alone knows the Father, and one cannot know God except through Jesus. Following this brief prayer of thanksgiving, Jesus turned to His disciples and posited their blessed privilege by stating that many prophets and kings had desired to see the things which they had seen.

2. *His Teachings Concerning Citizens of the Kingdom, 10:25-13:9*. This section is constituted by a series of teachings concerning the nature of the kingdom's citizens. If one is a citizen of the Messiah's kingdom, then certain characteristics are evident in his personal life.

(1) *Love of Neighbor, 10:25-37*. This teaching was occasioned by a lawyer who inquired of Jesus concerning the method of obtaining eternal life. The inquirer was a doctor of the law and skilled in its interpretation. Jesus answered his initial question with a question (10:26) which required a knowledge of the law to answer correctly. The lawyer then gave the rabbinic summary of Old Testament law— love to God and love to one's neighbor (Deuteronomy 6:5; Leviticus 19:18).

These details had been simple enough and were to have been expected by both parties. However, the lawyer was dissatisfied with the simplicity of Jesus' answer and sought to be more specific. His ulterior motives caused him to desire an answer making possible his evasion of Jesus' word. "Who is my neighbor?" was the most logical question to ask. Jesus answered the question by giving the parable of the Good Samaritan. Luke is the only gospel writer to include this parable in his material.

The parable concerns a certain man who traveled from Jerusalem to Jericho, an extremely dangerous journey. In a distance of approximately 17 miles the road drops some 3,600 feet. This narrow, rocky road with sharp corners and numerous hiding places for bandits was an ideal place for robbery. The traveler was robbed, stripped of his clothing, beaten, and left half-dead. Three men chanced to travel the same road that day. One was a priest who may have been returning to his home from his Temple responsibilities. This man saw the victim but simply passed by him. One was a Levite, who in all probability was also returning to his home from his Temple responsibilities in Jerusalem. He looked upon the victim but left him in his suffering and need, as had the priest. The third traveler was a hated Samaritan with whom no Jew would have social contact. Because of his ancestral difficulties with the Jew, no Samaritan of that generation could be accepted by a Jew. However, this Samaritan was not so uncouth as others had believed Samaritans to be. He had compassion for the robbery victim, ministering to his wounds and transporting him to an inn. There he "took care" of him. When the Samaritan left the inn on the following day, he paid for the victim's care and explained his willingness to accept the responsibility for additional care were the current payment not adequate.

The point had been made. Jesus simply asked, "Who was the neighbor?" The lawyer replied, "The one who made the mercy with him." Jesus then answered the lawyer's question, "Who is my neighbor?" by saying to him, "Go and you yourself *go on doing* in like manner." Thus the question was not, "Who was the neighbor?" but became, "Who acted as a neighbor is obligated to act?"

(2) *Importance of Hearing the Word, 10:38-42*. These verses further illustrate the truth of the previous section. In addition to illustrating love for one's neighbor, this section also illustrates the importance of hearing the word. Luke alone preserved this story.

John's gospel also reveals that Jesus made several journeys to Jerusalem in the few months prior to His crucifixion. It was likely on one of these journeys that this particular event occurred. The "certain village" (10:38) was Bethany, and the characters involved are the sisters of Lazarus. Jesus was a guest in Martha's home, and she was meticulously interested in providing for the guest's needs. Mary, the other sister, was more interested in what the guest could relate to her than she was in serving the guest. Martha became concerned by

Mary's indifference toward serving the Saviour and called this indifference to the Lord's attention. The Greek construction of the question is such as to expect an affirmative answer: "Lord, you do care that Mary does not assist me in serving, don't you?" Jesus answered by pointing out that Martha was concerned by many things, but one thing is supreme. Had He not suggested to Satan that man shall not live by bread alone? Service and care are essential, but one thing is supremely important. Mary had chosen that which was most important. Materialistic things could be removed, but the soul's worship of the Master is not altered even by death.

(3) *A Model Prayer, 11:1-13.* This prayer, along with the one recorded in Matthew 6:9-13, is often referred to as the "Lord's Prayer." Perhaps it is better to refer to this prayer as the "Model Prayer." The prayer of Jesus recorded in John 17 could more accurately be described as the Lord's Prayer.

Luke records the prayer during the extenuating circumstances of teaching the disciples to pray. They desired instruction in the same manner in which John had taught his disciples to pray. This request further reveals the inextricable interweaving of the ministries of John and Jesus.

Jesus addresses God as "Our Father" and describes Him as the One in Heaven. This is not suggestive of God's address but of His quality and character. God is Father, not in the sense of an adequate human fatherhood, but in the sense of a divine relationship with the Son. This address is normally employed by the Christian as he approaches the Father through the Son. The first section of the prayer concerns the Father as He and His kingdom are related to humanity. Jesus teaches His disciples to pray, "Let your name be sanctified." The name of God is to be set apart from all profane things. The Christian's relationship to the Father prompts him to recognize immediately the transcendence and holiness of God. This request is followed very closely by, "Thy will be done, as in heaven so in earth." When the Christian sanctifies the name of God and sets Him apart from all profane things, he becomes a part of the kingdom's coming in fulness. The suggestion, "Thy will be done, as in heaven so in earth," does not appear in the best texts of Luke's gospel, but it is in Matthew's account. For the kingdom of God to come in its fulness is tantamount to His will being done on earth, even as the angels perform His will in heaven. That Jesus dealt first with God, and man's relationship to Him, before He turned to the need of man is highly suggestive and significant.

Jesus portrays man's daily dependence upon God in the words, "Give us today our daily bread." Man's problems are innumerable; man's burdens are seldom related to one day. He chooses rather to collect them, reaching into the past and stretching into the future, then worrying about them all. Jesus simply states that man is to depend each day upon God's provision. This request for daily bread logically leads to a request for forgiveness of sins. But Jesus includes one aspect of forgiveness that the disciple seldom entertains—a suggestion that the disciple go on forgiving every obligation of man. To be forgiven, one must practice a spirit of forgiveness. He concludes the prayer with the request that God guard the individual against temptation ("do not ever begin to lead us into temptation"). James 1:13 reveals that God never entices man to sin, that sin comes from his own lust.

Jesus then gave two parables as encouragements to prayer. The first is concerned with persistence in prayer. It is the familiar account of a friend who visits his neighbor at midnight and requests some bread for the morning meal. A visitor has come to the friend's home and his provisions are thereby inadequate for the morning. Although the neighbor is reluctant to arise and disturb his sleeping family, he shares his food supply because of the friend's persistence. This encouragement is concluded by Jesus' observation in the form of a threefold promise. One continues asking, and it shall be given him. He continues seeking, and he shall find. He continues knocking, and it shall be opened to him. The tenses are present imperatives and avow the continuous action of the man. Asking, seeking, knocking —these guarantee success.

A second parable is equally brief and tells of a son who asks bread of his father. Although a flat stone resembles a loaf of bread, will the father give his son a stone? No! If the son requests a fish, will he give him a serpent? No! If he should ask an egg, will the father give his beloved son a scorpion? No! Jesus then concludes that God is more loving and wiser than man. If an evil man gives good gifts to his children, how much more the Heavenly Father is willing and anxious to give the Holy Spirit to those who ask Him. The bungling parent may make many mistakes, but he does the best that he can for his children. If he does his best, surely the omniscient Father will do even more!

(4) *A Question of Relationship to Beelzebub, 11:14-28.* The Jews believed in demons and also claimed to assert authority over them. In this section Luke describes the healing of a dumb demoniac

and the subsequent marveling of the people. The Jews did not question Jesus' ability to cast out demons, some suggesting that He did it through Beelzebub, the chief of the demons. This was equivalent to suggesting that He cast out demons through the power of Satan, the chief of the devils. In response to their thoughts, Jesus reminded the Jews that a kingdom divided against itself is brought to destruction; a divided house provides His illustration. This generalization had been observed by all His hearers; no argument against its veracity was advanced. Jesus then drew the analogy that Satan, divided against himself, would fall. Furthermore, He presumed for argument's sake that He had cast out devils by the power of Beelzebub. If so, through whom did their sons exorcise demons? On the other hand, if He cast out the demons through the power of God, then the kingdom of God must have been introduced into their midst.

This last assertion occasioned a brief observation concerning the robber of the palace. When a strong man guards the palace, his goods are safe; when one stronger comes and overpowers him, then the palace goods are divided as spoils. The palace can never be robbed until one stronger than the guard overpowers him. There can be no neutrality in this struggle with Satan (11:23). Man is either aligned with God or he is a victim of Satan.

The Jews of Jesus' day believed in the exorcism of demons and stated that when a rabbi drove a demon from a man, this was a sign of God's working through him. Yet, when Jesus performed such a miracle the Jews refused to ascribe this to God, assigning the act to the power of Satan. This statement made the Jews to be their own judges.

Jesus then described and illustrated spiritual cleansing by referring to the activities of an unclean spirit once he has been driven from a man. The demon walks through dry places seeking rest, but finding none, returns to his former abode. The house which he inhabited has been swept and cleaned. He enters again, taking with him seven spirits more wicked than himself. The last condition of the individual is worse than the former. By this teaching, Jesus is indicating the peril of an empty heart. Man's heart is no vacuum; it must be filled. When a man refuses to accept God's Spirit, he is practically inviting evil spirits to return. With their return, the man finds himself more helplessly under the influence of Satan than before. The idea of seven spirits suggests the conception of the completeness and wholeness of demonic possession. Neutrality toward Jesus is impossible. Either He fills the heart, or Satan does.

The accusation of Jesus' relationship to Beelzebub is broken in the text by the exclamation of a certain woman in the company who praised Mary for bearing Jesus. He did not criticize the woman's praise, but explained that the truly blessed individual is the one who hears the word of God and keeps it. Spiritual relationship to Jesus is more significant than physical relationship.

(5) *A Word Concerning a Sign, 11:29-36*. The Jews' quest to discern the true identity of Jesus is further suggested by their seeking a messianic sign. The sign might be the collapse of a wall in response to His command, the separation of the waters of the Jordan, or some similar sign indicative of divine relationship. On this occasion, Jesus reminded the assembled multitude that they were sign-seekers. The only sign to be given was the sign of Jonah. When compared to Matthew 12:40 ff., it becomes obvious that Jesus referred to His resurrection. The experience of Jonah served as a sign to the sinful Ninevites. Jonah appeared as one commissioned by God after having been saved from the great fish. The Son of Man by His resurrection will serve as a sign to His own sinful generation.

The Jews' rejection of Jesus' Messiahship prompted Him to remind them that the queen of the south (1 Kings 10) would condemn His contemporaries. She heard the wisdom of Solomon and believed him. But the Jews refused to believe Jesus, One greater than Solomon. Furthermore, the men of Nineveh joined in the condemnation of Jesus' generation, for they had repented upon hearing the preaching of Jonah. Jesus' own people refused His message. Jonah was an ordinary prophet; Jesus is the unique Son of God.

Jesus continues this emphasis (vss. 33-36). He is the "sign" of God. Employing the illustration of a candle, Jesus suggested that a candle is not hidden but it is placed upon a candlestick that it may light the entire room. Turning to an additional illustration, he defined the eye as the source of the body's light. If the eye presents a single image, the body is filled with light. If the eye presents a double image and one is hampered by spiritual astigmatism, then the body is filled with darkness.

(6) *A Denunciation of the Scribes and Pharisees, 11:37-54*. Luke here records a teaching of Jesus occasioned by a Pharisee's invitation to dinner. Jesus did not wash His hands ceremonially prior to the meal, and this astonished the Pharisee. His concern was unrelated to hygienic cleanliness; he was terribly upset because Jesus

had not washed His hands according to the precepts of ceremonial law. The teaching evoked by the Pharisee's reaction concerns pharisaic externalism. The Pharisees cleaned the outside of the cup and platter, but the inside was filled with wickedness. Jesus suggested that they kept the rabbinical law in all matters of externalism, but internally they were corrupt and rotten. They gave their alms as all good Jews should do. They divided all materials into clean and unclean portions. The tithing of mint, rue, and all manner of herbs was of utmost importance to them. But judgment and the love of God were meaningless. They desired the chief seats in the synagogues (those facing the worshipers) and honorific titles in market places. They were as unpainted graves by the roadside.

One student of the law objected to Jesus' reproach; this objection became the occasion for Jesus' teaching concerning lawyers. They were described as people who placed grievous burdens upon men, but the lawyers would not attempt to bear the burdens which they placed upon others. They built and maintained sepulchres for the prophets who had been killed by their own people. The persecution and subsequent execution of some of the prophets and apostles were not unknown to God, who held Jesus' generation responsible for their own evilness. Jesus indicated that the evil involved in the shedding of Abel's blood and that of Zacharias would be required of His generation. Abel's blood was the first shed according to the Old Testament record (Genesis 4:10), and Zacharias' the last in the Old Testament canon (II Chronicles 24:20-22). This series of six woes (vss. 42,43, 44,46,47,52) is concluded by the one pronounced upon the lawyers, who wore keys received from the Sanhedrin as indicative of their supposed ability to unlock the scriptures. In actuality, they had taken away the key of knowledge.

The brevity of Luke's conclusion further emphasizes the sadness of the denunciation. The scribes and Pharisees laid an ambush for Jesus, attempting to ensnare Him in His own words.

(7) *Teaching Concerning Personal Integrity, 12:1-13:9.* In these verses Jesus warned against the teachings of the Pharisees. He compared their teaching to leaven, which has a way of working itself throughout the dough. Jesus reminded His hearers that nothing is secret and that God is fully aware of all their actions and thoughts. God's omniscience is described by a reminder that He is fully aware of the sale of five sparrows for two farthings, even though sparrows are practically worthless. Jesus further reminded His hearers that the very hairs of their heads were numbered.

These verses are concluded by a statement concerning the un-
pardonable sin. The man who speaks injuriously against the Holy
Ghost shall not be forgiven. When a man becomes so degraded
spiritually that he cannot recognize the working of God and ascribes
that working to Satan, there is no moral hold to which God can grip.
Although some men may speak injuriously of Jesus and the working
of the Spirit, His followers may be assured of the Holy Spirit's
presence whenever they are arrested and brought before the magis-
trates. The Spirit shall teach them in that hour.

The disciple who requested his brother to divide his inheritance
with him provided the occasion for Jesus to speak the parable of the
rich fool. This is a parable underscoring the dangers of materialism.
The rich man's fields produced abundantly and he inquiringly faced
the question, "What shall I do, because I have no room wherein to
bestow my fruits?" His decision was simple but selfish: destroy his
present barns and build greater barns. This seemed reasonable, and
security seemed certain (12:19). The rich man could then live in
luxury and eat, drink, and be merry. But God's response was entirely
different; that night the rich man's soul was required of him. The
question remained, "Who would benefit from these possessions?" The
picture of covetousness is related forcefully in the words of this
parable. The man who had planned for the future in the terms of *"my*
barns, *my* fruits, *my* goods, and *my* soul" realized his folly only in
death. He left the world poorer than the destitute beggar on the busy
street corner. This is true of all who lay up treasures for themselves
without reference to God. Jesus did not condemn material possessions in this parable, nor did He condemn the desire to possess material things. However, He forcefully condemned covetousness and greed.

The foolishness of anxious concern for material possessions is
further discussed by Jesus (12:22-34). Life does not consist of material possessions; therefore, the disciple is "to take no thought for his
life, what he shall eat. . . ." Life is constituted by much more than the
eating of food and the wearing of clothing. Birds serve as an illustration of total dependence upon God's provisions. They are not knowl-
edgeable in sowing seed or reaping harvests; neither do they have a
storehouse or barn. Yet, God feeds them. Man is more significant
than the birds; therefore, he can logically depend upon God. Man
can worry, but his worry will not add to his stature. The term
"stature" refers either to physical height or physical life span. Worry
will not add to either. The beauty of the lilies is an illustration
employed by Jesus to indicate God's ability to provide clothing for

His people. The glory of Solomon was well known by every Jew, and Jesus reminded His hearers that Solomon in his glory was not attired as a lily. If God fashioned the lilies in such beauty and splendor, lilies which today exist in their beauty but tomorrow will be cast into the oven, does He not have a greater interest in providing for His people? The way of faith is to trust God and to depend upon his provision (vss. 29-30); the way of the world is distrust and disobedience. If God's claims occupy a place of priority, His people have no reason to fear inasmuch as He has promised them the kingdom (v. 32).

Personal integrity is also evident in one's readiness for the Lord's return. Jesus reminded His hearers that man's heart is lodged alongside his treasure. Spiritual integrity requires spiritual alertness and preparedness for the Lord's return. The disciple's loins are to be girded, no long flowing robes to trip him, and the lights of his house are to be burning expectantly as he awaits the Lord's return. Watchfulness and alertness bring blessing at the time of the advent. The indefiniteness of the advent is described by Jesus in His references to the second and third watches (v. 38). The disciple is to be alert regardless of the time of the Lord's return! If the owner of the house had known the hour of the thief's approach, he would have watched (v. 39). Jesus exhorted the disciples to be watchful because the Son of Man returns at an unexpected time, as does the thief who plunders the house.

The parable of the watchful servant prompted Peter to inquire concerning the individual or individuals addressed by Jesus (12:41). The Master replied that this parable was addressed to all who are His followers, but especially to those who occupy significant places of leadership. The faithful and watchful servant is the individual to whom the Lord grants a place of authority. The servant who is unattentive and irresponsible concerning the possibility of his Master's return lacks personal integrity, will be surprised by the Lord's sudden appearance, and will be separated from the Master's honored servants. His punishment will be great (v. 47) because his knowledge was great. He knew his Master's will, but refused to follow it. The principle of judgment according to light is delineated (v. 48) by Jesus' insistence that the man who knew not, but committed things worthy of stripes, will be beaten with few stripes.

Man's personal integrity is demanded by the disciple's personal relationship to Jesus (vss. 49-59). Jesus' ministry is one of spiritual fire; it is divisive in its nature. Fire consumes the destructible, but at the same time purifies and refines the indestructible. Jesus recognized an eternal purpose (v. 50) but also visualized the divisive effect of His ministry (v. 51). The truth proclaimed by Jesus creates division within the household and within the family (vss. 52-53).

The lack of personal integrity in the life of the Jew is illustrated by his inability to discern the signs of his time. Although he had the ability to observe the cloud rising out of the west and thereby predict a shower, or the blowing of the south wind and then predict intense heat, he lacked the ability to consider the spiritual events and thereby define the spiritual time.

Jesus' hearers had failed to recognize the impending judgment of God. They had also failed to recognize the revelation of God provided in the person of His Son. Jesus' closing counsel was couched in words relating the experience of a man and his enemy. It was Jesus' suggestion that he be reconciled to the adversary, lest the adversary bring the man before the judge, and the judge deliver him to the officer, who in turn would cast him into prison. The story is couched in physical terminology but relates spiritual truth. The man who fails to be reconciled to God through Jesus must pay the price for his sins. The future is indeed bleak.

The final section concerning personal integrity is constituted by the terse statements of 13:1-9. Luke does not identify the particular time or occasion for Pilate's slaying some Galileans who were sacrificing to God (vss. 1-3); the author merely mentions that Pilate mingled their blood with the blood of their sacrifices. Is it possible that these Galileans were those "who missed the mark more extensively" than all other sinners? Is their suffering indicative that they alone disobeyed God? The Master emphatically answered, "No!" All men will perish apart from repentance. Again it must be remembered that repentance is no mere sorrow but a decisive turning from sin, a change of attitude, the assuming of a loyalty to God. The necessity of repentance for all who wish to enter the kingdom is further illustrated by a reference to the 18 men who perished in the fall of Siloam's tower (13:4-5). This tower was likely located near the pool of Siloam, which was situated at an angle where the southern and eastern walls of the ancient city joined. This incident is mentioned nowhere else, but Jesus used it as an illustration of the necessity of repentance for all people. Surely these 18 were not the only sinners who lived in Jerusalem! Jesus indicated that all would perish unless they repented of their sin.

The brief parable of the barren fig tree concludes this section. The parable illustrates the teaching defined in the accounts of the executed Galileans and the 18 men who were killed in the collapse of Siloam's tower. A man planted a fig tree; during a period of three years he sought fruit from its branches but found none. The owner then addressed the keeper of the vineyard and commanded him to cut down the tree; it occupied good soil in which a fruitful tree could be planted. The keeper of the vineyard reminded the owner that he would be happy to dig around the roots and fertilize it. If the tree did not then bear fruit, he would destroy it as the owner had insisted. In this parable Jesus refers to barren Israel, who had enjoyed many opportunities to bear fruit but had remained barren. The parable suggests that God would give the Jews one additional opportunity to bear fruit. If the nation continued in her disobedience and rebellion, it would then be removed from its honored position as God's chosen people.

3. *His Teachings Concerning the Kingdom, 13:10-22.* This general section contains numerous teachings concerning the kingdom and the nature of its citizens. It is likewise the parable section of the gospel, and from this standpoint is somewhat analogous to Matthew 13.

(1) *Healing the Cripple on a Sabbath, 13:10-17.* The one who received the benefits of this miracle was a woman who had possessed a physical infirmity for 18 years. Her body was drawn; Luke here employs a medical word which describes the curvature of the spine. She was helpless, unable even to lift herself. Jesus saw her physical condition and called her, saying, "Woman thou art loosed from thine infirmity." He laid His hands on her; she was immediately healed and her body straightened. She "kept on glorifying" God. The ruler of the synagogue, the head of the ten men controlling the local institution, was angered by Jesus' action. His anger was occasioned by the fact that a miracle had been performed on the Sabbath, not by the fact that the woman's body had been healed. The legalism of the law emphasized that man has six days in which to work. Jesus could perform His acts of mercy within that period of time and not on the Sabbath. Jewish hypocrisy was revealed in the fact that not one of them would refuse to loose an animal from his stall and water him on the Sabbath, but their legalism prevented their willingness to accept such a miracle on the Sabbath. This woman was of far greater value than the animal which was cared for routinely on the Sabbath. The sharpness of Jesus' words put His adversaries to shame, and as they were ashamed the people "were continuing to rejoice" because of the glorious things effected by Jesus.

The compassionate Jesus created further problems with His adversaries but experienced still additional appreciation on the part of His friends.

(2) *The Parables of the Mustard Seed and Leaven, 13:18-22.* The vastness and rapidity of the kingdom's growth is illustrated by the grain of mustard seed planted in the garden. The seed was the smallest planted by farmers in Palestine, and yet upon germination developed into the largest Palestinian plant grown from a seed. Jesus adds that the mustard plant becomes large enough for birds to find lodging in its branches. The point made by the Master concerns the growth of the kingdom. Even though the kingdom may have a small beginning, His disciples are not to be dismayed by the smallness of beginning; they are to understand that as the small mustard seed develops into an impressive plant, even so the kingdom grows rapidly and to immense proportions.

The parable of the leaven is also designed to illustrate the growth of the kingdom (vss. 20-21). Perhaps the parable of the mustard seed illustrates the external growth of the kingdom; if so, the parable of the leaven illustrates the internal development of the kingdom. When the yeast is put into the dough, it permeates the material until the whole mass is leavened. As the small mustard seed develops into a plant of eight to twelve feet in height and as a little yeast permeates three measures of meal, even so does the kingdom of God continue to develop within the hearts of men, as well as in external proportions. Once the yeast has begun to permeate the dough, its progress is not halted. Nor can one stop the growth of the kingdom.

FOR FURTHER STUDY

1. Read the article entitled "Scribe" in *The New Smith's Bible Dictionary*, pp. 340-341.

2. How does the work of a scribe compare with that of a minister?

3. Define some of the characteristics of Jesus' teachings. What makes Him the teacher all seek to emulate?

4. Read the article entitled "The Kingdom of God" in *The Zondervan Pictorial Bible Dictionary*, pp. 466-467. What makes Matthew's attitude toward the kingdom unique?

5. Read the article entitled "The Law of the Sabbath" in *The Interpreter's Dictionary of the Bible*, pp. 135-141. Why was healing a violation of Sabbath law?

6. What does the parable of the mustard seed mean to a contemporary Christian?

CHAPTER SEVEN

Numerous Teachings Along the Way

A Jewish rabbi customarily taught his disciples either while in a structured teaching situation or while strolling along the roadway. It was not unusual for a noted rabbi to be accompanied by a large group. This portion of the gospel records some of the teachings given by Jesus as the band of disciples journeyed toward Jerusalem. Some of the choice parables of His ministry were related during this time.

1. *Concerning Discipleship, 13:23-14:35.* The previous parables indicate that the kingdom will be victorious, but Jesus recognized that it would be difficult for some to accept the kingdom.

(1) *Requirements in Discipleship Essential to the Kingdom, 13:23-35.* The disciples were also cognizant of the difficulty with which many would approach the kingdom and thus inquired of Jesus, "Are they few that shall be saved?" Jesus did not answer the question theoretically; He insisted that man strive to enter the kingdom (the term itself means "to be intent as one struggles for a prize in athletic contests"). Luke uses a similar word, *agonia* (22:44), to describe the struggle of Jesus in Gethsemane. The strait gate is the only means of entering the kingdom, and few will be able to enter even though many may attempt to find it. The essentials of kingdom citizenship are defined by God, not man. Jesus demonstrates the abuse of opportunity by referring to the householder who had closed his door for the night. The frustrated and false hopes held by those outside will become judgments upon them. Their own confessions remind them of wasted opportunities (vss. 26-27).

Spiritual agonizing follows when one realizes that he has neglected his opportunities to enter the kingdom. These same Jews who have refused all invitations and opportunities will be further chagrined by seeing Abraham, Isaac, Jacob, and all the prophets in the kingdom of

God. The Jews would normally claim spiritual relationship to God by virtue of physical relationship to Abraham. That some of Jesus' contemporaries refused His kingdom does not alter the fact that men shall come from the four corners of the earth to occupy places within the kingdom of God (v. 29). The sadness and remorse of the hour is made more acute by the recognition that some who are first (Jews) shall be last, and some of the last (Gentiles) shall be first.

The requirements of discipleship were further taught by Jesus' reply to certain of the Pharisees who warned Him of the animosity of Herod Antipas toward Him. They were possibly interested in Jesus' welfare; however, some interpreters suggest that the Pharisees were interested in Jesus' leaving their area and traveling to an area where the Jewish rulers would be sure to capture Him. The stringent requirements of the kingdom apply not only to the citizens, but also to its king. Jesus replied that He would continue His ministry and on the third day would be perfected. He referred to Herod as a "fox," a wise but weak ruler. The third day is likely a reference to His sufferings. He reiterated (v. 33) the teaching in the words, "I must walk today, and tomorrow, and the day following: for it cannot be that a prophet perish out of Jerusalem." Jesus recognized God's will and God's moving in history. He fully realized that He would not give His life outside the city of Jerusalem.

The mention of Jerusalem was an occasion for great lamentation. The obstinacy of Jerusalem had touched Jesus' heart. Jesus had desired to protect Jerusalem as a hen might protect the chicks; nevertheless, Jerusalem was unwilling to maintain this relationship. Her refusal meant total destruction and desolation. The Jews could reject Jesus in His earthly ministry, but some day along with all men they would pronounce Him blessed.

(2) *Another Sabbath Healing Followed by Two Parables, 14:1-24.* Luke first mentioned the journeys to Jerusalem in 9:51. Chapter 14 begins a second section of material dealing with the journeys. In the section extending from 14:1 to 17:10 and containing material essentially unique to Luke, the historian gives personal insights and glimpses into this period of the Saviour's ministry. This section is introduced by an account of another conflict with the Pharisees. Jesus had been invited into the home of a chief Pharisee, one of the leading exponents of pharisaism. It was a Sabbath and the Pharisees carefully observed Jesus' every action in an attempt to discover His appreciation for Sabbath law. A man who suffered from dropsy was present and afforded an opportunity for Jesus to question

the lawyers and Pharisees. The ageless question concerning healing on the Sabbath was raised, but the Pharisees wisely refused to comment. Jesus then healed the dropsied man and justified His action on the basis of humaneness. He reminded the Pharisees that they would care for an ass or an ox which had fallen into a pit on a Sabbath. To this argument they had no answer.

Jesus then related a parable rebuking social pride. The guests of the leading Pharisee were vying for the chief seats—the seat to the right of the host was of primary significance, the seat to the host's immediate left was secondary, and the positions then alternated in order of importance. The place of honor was assigned an individual because of the host's evaluation of his person. The same remains true in the Lord's evaluation of man's character. Verse 11 succinctly summarizes the parable and indicates that the person exalting himself in this life will be humiliated in the Lord's presence, but the person who humbles himself in this life shall be exalted by the Lord.

Jesus then turned to His host and suggested that his guest list should include not only friends, relatives, and neighbors but should also include the poor, the maimed, the lame, and the blind. Those of the latter categories will not be able to return the favor, but the Lord will bless the host in the resurrection of the just.

These words of Jesus evoked a response from one of the guests who said, "Blessed is he that shall eat bread in the kingdom of God" (v. 15). This man voiced a prevalent Jewish idea concerning a great and extended feast to be held in the Messianic Age. Using this observation as a springboard for additional teaching, Jesus then gave the parable of the great supper. When the meal was prepared and all in readiness, the host sent his servant to the invited guests to indicate that all was prepared. However, the invited guests began to offer excuses. When the servant returned with these reports, his lord became angry and instructed the servant to go into the streets and invite the poor, the maimed, the halt, and the blind. Having acted obediently, the servant then reported that he had fulfilled the master's command but additional room was available. The lord then said to his servant, "Go into the highways and hedges and compel them to come in, that my house may be filled."

This parable obviously portrays an invitation to the messianic kingdom and illustrates the fact that some may refuse the kingdom but others will enter by invitation. However, an invitation alone is not adequate; one must accept the invitation.

(3) *The Cost of Kingdom Discipleship, 14:25-35.* Any miracle worker could attract multitudes, and unquestionably many people followed Jesus because of His miraculous power. Yet, Jesus' intent and purpose was to define the cost of true discipleship that His followers might understand the price of His yoke. True discipleship involves total and complete loyalty to the Master (v. 26). No loyalty can take precedence over loyalty to Christ, not even loyalty to one's parents or immediate family. The disciple must be willing to bear his cross; apart from cross-bearing, there is no discipleship (v. 27).

Jesus suggested the logic of one's counting the cost of discipleship by illustrations concerning building and warfare. The building of a tower is costly, as is the waging of a war. If the contractor does not count the cost, he may be unable to complete the structure. If the king does not number his soldiers and those of his enemy, he may act wiser in seeking peace rather than conflict. Discipleship means the renunciation of selfish interest and the acceptance of God's will (v. 33), although there is a cost to be considered.

If the disciple is to flavor society, then he must possess the special qualities and characteristics of true discipleship. Salt is worthless if it is tasteless. The man with ability to understand spiritual truth is warned by these words of Jesus.

2. *A Series of Parables, 15:1-17:10.* Matthew's gospel is remembered for its record of the words of Jesus. However, Luke relates much of Jesus' parabolic material. Several of the parables contained in this section are unique to Luke's gospel.

(1) *The Concern of God for the Lost, 15:1-32.* The parables of this chapter illustrate God's concern for those separated from Him. The Father is unwilling for any to perish.

a. *The Lost Sheep, 15:1-7.* The parable is also contained in Matthew (18:12 ff.). Both gospels use this parable as an illustration of God's concern for the lost. Luke indicates that Jesus' hearers were publicans (tax collectors) and sinners. The Pharisees joined the scribes in criticizing Jesus for His contact with the social and religious outcasts, suggesting that He received sinners and socialized with them.

Jesus then related the account of a shepherd who cared for 100 sheep. However, upon counting them he learned that one sheep was missing; he left the 99 to search for the one which was lost. This action well illustrates the shepherd's care for *one.* Verse 5 suggests that the shepherd also rejoiced in finding the lost sheep.

Jesus explained the teaching of the parable (v. 7), suggesting that heaven knows more joy because of the repentance of one sinner than because of 99 who need no repentance. Jesus firmly stated that God is concerned with one person who is lost and is not simply concerned with a man who is legalistically and rabbinically correct.

b. *The Lost Coin, 15:8-10.* This brief parable relates the story of a woman possessing ten pieces of silver. She lost one coin, lit a candle, and swept the house until she had found the lost coin. Having found the coin, she called her friends and neighbors and shared her joy with them. The *one* lost coin had brought sorrow; finding the *one* lost coin brought joy.

c. *The Lost Son, 15:11-32.* This story contains numerous spiritual truths and is described by some interpreters as the "gospel within the gospel." The main characters of the story are a father and his two sons. One son remained with the father; the other son strayed into a foreign land. Both sons, however, were separated from the father's love. The pathos of sin and guilt likewise enter the details of the story, but the account ends on a happy note with the return of the lost son and the reinstitution of both sons into the father's graces.

The younger son desired his inheritance that he might make his own life in the land of his choice. He soon journeyed to another country, where he wasted his inheritance. After squandering all his possessions, he experienced an extensive famine and had nothing to satisfy the requirements of his body. Joining himself to a foreigner's household, he found employment in caring for the foreigner's swine. His only food was that of the swine. The son, nevertheless, eventually realized his condition and turned from his waywardness to remember the position of his father's hired servants. His great decision (v. 18) came in his willingness to return to his father and admit that he had sinned against God and wished only to be considered a servant of his father. In this spirit he returned to his father, who obviously was watching for his son. The father ran to meet him and bestowed kisses of love and appreciation upon his brow. The son then confessed his sinfulness and admitted that he was unworthy to be considered the son of his father's household.

The father's response was what one would expect of the Heavenly Father. This father received his son into his household; he placed a robe around his body, a ring on his hand, and shoes on his feet. Finally, he issued orders for a feast of thanksgiving. His son who had been dead now lived; he had been lost, now he has been found. Rejoicing and happiness express the delight of the scene.

The father's forgiveness of the second son was more than adequate. The older son expressed intense displeasure at his father's attitude toward his brother (vss. 28-29). He reminded his father of the long days of faithful service which he had given in utter devotion and obedience; he also noted his father's apparent neglect. He pointed to the apparent inconsistency of his father's action by reminding him that his brother had already spent his inheritance in sinful living. The father's response was one of tenderness and compassion; he reminded the faithful son that he shared with him all his possessions, and that it was only fitting that they rejoice in the return of the prodigal.

The details of the story speak volumes of truth. To note only the detail which describes human pathos, suffering, and compassion is to fail to find the point illustrated by Jesus. Obviously, the son who strays from home depicts a sinner separated from God. The prodigal's sin is not involved simply in the waste of his inheritance or in his careless attitudes and behavior. It is a sin of a debauched life, a rebellion against love. The account well illustrates the fall of man (Genesis 3:5). The love of God is seen in the activity of the father. When the son returned to his father, it was not for the purpose of gaining a new inheritance but for the expressed purpose of becoming an obedient servant. Such repentance brings forgiveness. The father was not merely accepting the son as a servant but was restoring him as a son, inasmuch as slaves wore no shoes.

Perhaps the life of the older brother illustrates the animosity and misunderstanding of the Pharisees. He did not understand his father's forgiveness and grace. The older brother believed his past service had brought him into a proper relationship with the father; he believed himself to be more acceptable than the prodigal. Yet, his definition of sonship was as perverted as that of the prodigal. Having remained with his father and within his father's household, he had failed to understand the true spirit existing between father and son. Because of this, he found it impossible to comprehend his father's joy in the return of the sinful brother.

God's concern for the lost is illustrated in the parable of the prodigal. Jesus welcomed publicans and sinners into His kingdom, although the Pharisees and scribes questioned His social and religious contact with them.

(2) *The Concern for the Christian's Stewardship, 16:1-17:10.* God is not only concerned for those separated from Him; He is also interested in the stewardship of the Christian.

a. *The Dishonest Steward, 16:1-13.* This parable defines selfishness and injustice in dealing with possessions belonging to another, the steward's master. The steward was a house manager, responsible for the goods of the master. This particular steward was slandered; he was accused of wasting his lord's goods. The master called him and required an account of his stewardship. The accusations brought against this steward proved to be true. He faced the dilemma of having his stewardship taken from him and then having no employment. He was unwilling to accept hardship and toil as his way of life, and he was ashamed to beg.

Acting adroitly and wisely, he called those indebted to his master and inquired of their indebtedness. When each debtor acknowledged a given indebtedness, the steward then suggested that the bill be decreased by a considerable amount. When the master learned of the steward's action, he acknowledged the wisdom thereof, admitting that the steward had acted cleverly.

Jesus used these words to illustrate the wisdom with which men of the world conduct themselves and provide for their futures (v. 8b). Jesus taught His disciples to make friends of the "mammon of unrighteousness" that they may be received by those able to provide materially for them. Jesus did not commend dishonest methods. He did suggest that the men of the world acted more wisely in providing for the future than those of spiritual sensitivity. By this parable, Jesus suggested that the Christian could be prudent and wise in the usage of his possessions for the benefit of others. This does not mean that an individual is admitted to heaven because he has given generously. Heaven belongs to a man because of his relationship to God, and it is this relationship which prompts the Christian to be a good steward of his possessions. Verse 13 summarizes Jesus' teaching. The inability of men to be obedient to two diverse masters is clearly stated. Man cannot be double-minded. Jesus bluntly concluded, "Ye cannot serve God and mammon." But you can serve God by using possessions in a spiritual fashion.

b. *The Criticism of the Pharisees, 16:14-18.* The Pharisees were fraternal in spirit and prided themselves in their kindly treatment of one another. Yet, Jesus described them as covetous (v. 14). They were extremely greedy, not only for position but likewise for riches. Jesus indicated (v. 15) that they sought to justify themselves before men in the meticulous keeping of the law. The Pharisees made the mistake of retaining the ceremonial law and failing to understand that the law and the prophets pointed to the ministry of the Saviour.

Following the time of John the Baptizer, the kingdom of God was preached and men pressed into the kingdom. Jesus recognized again the eternal quality and verity of the law; He pointed out that the appearance of a new order with John and Jesus in no fashion abrogated the previous revelation of God. Yet, the Pharisees erred in setting the ceremonial and rabbinical law against the law of God in Christ. Illustration of the permanence of the law is seen in Jesus' reference to adultery; adultery remained adultery even though the messianic dispensation had come. Jesus (Matthew 5:17) indicated that the law was to be honored and that He Himself had no intention of destroying the law but purposed to live "in the law" so that its deepest realities might be seen.

c. *The Rich Man and Lazarus, 16:19-31.* Stewardship of life was further enforced by Jesus in the account of Dives and Lazarus. The Pharisees acknowledged materialistic possessions as a sign of God's blessings and poverty as a sign of God's judgment.

The familiar account describes a certain rich man, clothed in purple and fine linen. He obviously attired his body in the clothing of royalty and seemed to entertain constantly with sumptuous banquets. A second character was described as a beggar named Lazarus, whose body was covered with sores and who lay daily at the gate of the rich man's palace. The beggar desired the crumbs which fell from the rich man's table. He had no friends to love and care for him; dogs, the scavengers of the first century world, took an interest in him and licked his sores.

The account shifts from a description of the characters to the experience of death. The beggar died and angels carried him "into Abraham's bosom," a favorite Jewish expression for God. The rich man died and was buried; likely his burial was an extravagant service. However, he is described as being in hell, where he lifted his eyes and observed the heavenly scene of Lazarus in the Father's bosom. The rich man cried to father Abraham and begged for mercy, pleading that Lazarus might bring just a drop of water to cool his tongue. He was tormented by the flame and agony of the terrible place.

The third character then spoke. Abraham replied to the rich man, "Son, remember that thou in thy lifetime receivedst thy good things, and likewise Lazarus evil things. . . ." The Jewish conception of the Fatherhood of God is expressed in the term "Son." This term of kindness and endearment prepares the reader for the sad words to follow. Things could not be altered from their current conditions, inasmuch as each man made an eternal choice prior to the experience of death. Were this not enough, father Abraham declared that an impassable gulf was established between the rich man and the poor beggar.

The rich man then insisted that Lazarus be sent to his five brothers to warn them of the agony of the place of torment. Father Abraham replied that the brothers had Moses and the prophets to relate the conditions of responsibility and duty. The rich man continued his arguments, pointing out that one from the dead would be more impressive than the law and the prophets. But father Abraham declared with finality that the brothers would not be disposed to hear Lazarus if they would not hear the instructions of Moses and the prophets.

The selfish, wordly life of the rich man well illustrates the general conceptions and attitudes of the Pharisees. This man had not gone to hell because of wealth, but because of his failure to acknowledge the lordship of Jesus. Poverty does not automatically bring eternal joy, nor does wealth automatically commit one to hell. The future depends upon man's relationship to God, a relationship reflected in his attitude toward his life and possessions. The Pharisees had continued in their greed and thus continued in danger of final separation from God, although they claimed their material possessions to be an evidence of God's favor and blessings.

d. *The Dangers of Negative Attitudes, 17:1-4.* Jesus admitted that offenses would come to the Christian, but He pronounced a woe upon the individual through whom the offense came. Jesus indicated that it would be better for the offender to have a millstone hanged about his neck and be cast into the sea than for him to become a stumbling block to the Christian. Sin is not committed in a vacuum; therefore, man's sin affects other Christians. This principle of care in dealing with others is further illustrated by the suggestion that the Christian forgive his brother. The Christian may call the brother's trespass to his attention, but he is obligated to forgive the brother. Although the Jews believed seven times to be ample forgiveness, the Christian is to know no limit in his forgiveness of others.

e. *The Unprofitable Servant, 17:5-10.* The transition between the previous section and the account of the unprofitable servant lacks smoothness. When the apostles requested Jesus to increase their faith, Jesus then reminded them that even with a small faith one is able to remove many obstacles that possibly stand between his soul and victory in God's purpose. The smallness of this faith was illustrated by the grain of mustard seed which germinates and develops into an herb so large the birds can find places of lodging. The disciples' faith, if it contained that vitality and vigor, could result in equally great accomplishments. It is the quality of faith and not the amount of faith which Jesus declared to be important. The disciples did not need a "larger" faith; they needed a deeper faith.

The parable of the unprofitable servant relates the story of a servant performing the menial tasks about the farm. When he has completed these tasks, the master does not believe himself to be subservient because of the servant's obedience, nor does he feel any sense of obligation to thank the servant for performing the tasks assigned him.

The steward's obligation to God exceeds any obligation to himself. Having performed that which God expects of him, the steward can only remind himself that he too is an unprofitable servant. God's rewards, whatever they may be, are of grace and not of merit.

FOR FURTHER STUDY

1. Review Luke's record of Jesus' parables.
2. Why did Jesus employ parables?
3. Read A. M. Hunter's *Interpreting the Parables,* pp. 7-41, for some helpful insights into the parabolic method and the interpretation of parables.
4. Using a concordance, compare Paul's teachings concerning stewardship with that of Jesus in Luke 16:1-13.
5. Compare Jesus' teachings in Matthew 5:21-48 and Luke 17:1-4. Note His teachings concerning one's attitude.

CHAPTER EIGHT

Last Events of the Journey

Luke 9:51 introduces the journeys to Jerusalem, and Luke 17:11 introduces the last of the journeys. Jesus' ministry, even during its concluding aspects, continued to be characterized by numerous teachings and miracles. The sovereignty of Jesus is underscored in the major portion of this section (18:15-19:28). He had earlier established Himself as the Lord of history. In the concluding segments of His public ministry He further emphasized His lordship.

1. *The Healing of Ten Lepers, 17:11-19.* In this account, Luke continues to emphasize the potential dangers relating to a disciple and his stewardship. This story concerns ten lepers who conducted themselves according to the precepts of Jewish law (cf. Luke 5:12-16; Leviticus 13:45-46). Upon seeing Jesus they begged Him to have mercy on them. Luke's description suggests that they cried aloud as "an animal might howl because of the light of the moon." On this occasion there is no record of the Master's touching the lepers; He merely commanded them to show themselves unto the priests. It is to be understood that this was in keeping with the Levitical law concerning cleansing and the necessary offerings accompanying healing (Leviticus 14:2-8). One of them returned to Jesus and in a loud voice glorified God for this personal cleansing and purification. The leper fell on his face and continued thanking Him.

The significant thing concerning this man's gratitude is his racial identification—he was a Samaritan, not a Jew. Luke indicates that the Samaritan did that which was right in expressing gratitude (cf. the parable of the Good Samaritan, Luke 10:25-37). Perhaps one should understand that the nine were Jews and had been in the Samaritan's company only because all ten were lepers. Lepers often sought consolation and comfort by joining themselves to others of similar condition. Yet, only the lowly Samaritan returned to express appreciation for personal healing.

95

Nothing does more to prostitute and frustrate one's stewardship of life than the sin of ingratitude. The question "where are the nine?" remains pertinent to the ingratitude of a twentieth century society.

2. *A Word Concerning the Parousia, 17:20-37.* These verses provide several insights into the nature of the kingdom, the suddenness of the parousia, the conditions of the world at the time of the Saviour's return, and the final and complete separation of good and evil. The discussion was occasioned by the Pharisees, who constantly thought of the kingdom in terms of the Messiah's advent. No question occupied more of their thought or demanded a greater portion of their energies than the time of the Saviour's coming. Given an opportune moment, the Pharisees asked Jesus to reveal the time of the kingdom's coming. He again replied that the kingdom does not come with outward observation, but its manifestation is internal and heartfelt. That man does not point and exclaim, "There is the kingdom!" is plainly stated (v. 21). The kingdom of God was already in their midst, but these people failed to recognize its presence inasmuch as they had prejudged the nature of the kingdom. From His word to the Pharisees concerning the time of the kingdom's establishment, Jesus turned to give His attention to the suddenness of His return. His return was to be preceded by times when His people would earnestly desire to see the Son of Man (v. 22); it would likewise be preceded by the appearance of false teachers and pseudomessiahs who would claim personal followings. However, the return of the Lord is to be as sudden and decisive as the lightning which flashes from one segment of the sky to another. The lightning appears in the sudden flash to all men, and the Son of Man's return will be equally visible and will appear with equal suddenness. Prior to His return, Jesus must suffer many things and be rejected by His own people (v. 25). The conditions of the world at the return of the Lord will be similar to those in the days of Noah (v. 26). Routine and human activities also characterized the days of Lot. When Lot left Sodom, fire and brimstone rained from heaven upon the evil city. These are to be the conditions prior to the advent of Christ (vss. 28-30). The solemn reminder (remember Lot's wife) recalled a tragedy enacted in the life of one who had fled Sodom but still wished to remain attached to the evil city. Jesus concluded this section of His teaching concerning the parousia by repeating a gospel paradox: The one who selfishly saves life shall lose it, but the one who unselfishly loses life shall preserve it.

Just as the advent occurs in decisiveness, so will a decisive separation occur at the time of the Lord's return. The separation of good and evil was suggested by Jesus in the statement that two men may sleep in one bed, but one will be taken and the other left. Two women may be involved in the grinding of grain; one shall be taken, the other left. Two men may be involved in routine agricultural activities, but one will be taken and the other left. These illustrations prompted the question, "But where, Lord?" Jesus' answer is likely couched in the words of a popular proverb of the day: "Wheresoever the body is, thither will the eagles be gathered together." The proverb teaches that where conditions of decay exist, judgment is sure to follow. Where bodies are decayed physically, vultures gather; where men are decayed spiritually, judgment follows.

3. *Additional Teaching Concerning Prayer, 18:1-14.* These two parables actually relate to the teachings of the last section, and further teach that prayer is the best way to avoid succumbing to the temptations previously mentioned (17:20-37).

(1) *The Parable of the Widow and the Judge, 18:1-8.* The parable is set in an undefined city, and the judge is unidentified. He is described as a godless man who did not honor the dignity of humanity. Neither is the widow identified, but her request is. She asked the judge to avenge her of her adversary. The judge at first refused to heed the woman's request, but later yielded because of the widow's persistence (vss. 4-5). Jesus then related that God hears prayers and avenges His own because of their persistence. The question which haunted Jesus was, "Would the Son of Man find faith similar to the widow's when He returns?"

No one is able to know the time of the Lord's return, but everyone is able to be prepared spiritually for that return. It may seem as if the parousia is delayed; but Jesus insists that His followers continue in prayer, recognizing that He will return at the proper time and in the proper manner. Although the character of the judge stands in sharp contrast to the character of God the Father, Jesus wishes His followers to know that God hears persistent prayer just as the judge was moved by the persistency of the widow.

(2) *The Parable of the Pharisee and the Publican, 18:9-14.* This familiar parable does not relate to persistence or to faith as such, but specifically to the attitude in which one offers his prayers. Two men are depicted in prayer; one is a Pharisee, the other a publican. The legalistic Pharisee stood and thanked God that he was not an extortioner, an unjust man, an adulterer, or even as this tax collector who

stood by him. The pious Pharisee was proud of his holiness as measured by legalistic and external standards. Of course, as a Pharisee he tithed his possessions. In other words, he was a good Pharisee; tithing and fasting constituted important aspects of his life.

On the other hand, the publican was conscious of his sin and stood at a distance from the Pharisee. His humility is indicated by his refusal to lift his eyes to heaven and in the constant striking of his breast, saying, "God be merciful to me, *the* sinner." The publican had nothing to recommend himself except his humility and honesty. Jesus said that the publican was justified, the Pharisee was not. Self-exaltation brings humiliation, but humility results in exaltation. Righteousness is not external but internal. God's mercy belongs to the man who humbles himself.

4. *The Sovereignty of the Saviour, 18:15-19:28.* Luke selects several incidents which reveal the sovereignty of the Lord and indicate the eternal wisdom which He employed in digressing from the social and religious customs of His day.

(1) *In Receiving the Children, 18:15-17.* Luke's brief account (cf. Matthew 19:13 ff. and Mark 10:13 ff.) relates that some of the Jews brought their children to Jesus on a particular occasion. These folk seemingly desired nothing but the blessings of the Saviour for their children. Jesus called them alongside Him and said to His disciples, "Permit the little children to come unto me, and stop forbidding them; for of people of this character is the kingdom of heaven." He then stated an acceptance and wholeheartedness of commitment similar to that of a child are essential for entry into the kingdom. Jesus did not regard the blessing of the children as a waste of time or a frustration of purpose. Rather, He employed this social experience as a background for reminding His hearers that humility and simple faith are characteristic of the kingdom's citizens. The child trusts, is loyal, and accepts without question that which is done for him. By these words, Jesus insists that man is to accept with equal simplicity what God has done for him. Apart from these conditions it is *impossible* to enter God's kingdom.

(2) *In Declaring the Necessity of Total Commitment, 18:18-30.* The Lord's sovereignty in relationship to total commitment and its requirements is illustrated in these verses. Luke alone records that this man occupied a place of importance among the Jews. The young man came to Jesus and sincerely asked the way to inherit eternal life. He had likely inherited his wealth; and to him, inheritance seemed to

be the only way one gained a thing of value. If the inheritance of eternal life required an expenditure of money, this man stood ready to purchase life. Jesus turned the point of the conversation by inquiring: "Why callest thou me good? None is good, save one, that is God." God is the only One who is good in the absolute sense. If, therefore, the young man recognized Jesus only as a human teacher, he had no right to use the term "good" in his address of Jesus. Jesus did not deny His own goodness, but probed the depths of the man's heart in an attempt to inspire a correlation between the Father and the Son. Jesus repeated the commandments, only to have the youth indicate that he had kept his commandments all his life. Jesus then moved directly to the point without arguing the youth's ability to have kept the commandments and suggested that the young man lacked one thing: The youth's possessions stood between him and the kingdom. He was commanded to sell all that he had, distribute the money to the poor, and follow the Saviour. Having heard this, the young man became very sorrowful; he was *very rich* (a multimillionaire in our parlance). Jesus then noted that it is difficult for a rich man to depend upon one other than himself. Just as it would be impossible for a camel to pass through the eye of a needle, even so it is impossible humanly for a rich man to enter the kingdom of God. Whether the needle refers to a needle-like gate in the city wall or a sewing needle, and whether the term "camel" should be "rope" (a term closely akin in Greek) makes little difference. Jesus is pointing to the extreme difficulty of a wealthy man's coming to depend upon a person other than himself. The disciples then inquired concerning who could be saved. Jesus indicated that the salvation of the rich is possible with God, although their willingness to depend upon fellow man is almost incomprehensible. His answer suggests that God's sacrifice has been offered for all men, rich and poor alike.

This life illustration reveals the danger of trusting in self. This young man had trusted in himself, his wealth, his achievements, and had refused to trust God. Jesus showed that the man himself was the center of life instead of God by commanding him to sell his possessions and become a follower of the Master. Although it is difficult for man to be released from self, Jesus' answer to the disciples (v. 27) states God's ability to release man from that which keeps him from God.

If self-trust is despicable, then Peter wished to know the value of self-sacrifice (vss. 28-30). Jesus replied that self-sacrifice is profitable and that no individual goes unrewarded for his sacrificial service.

He indicated that one would receive manifold for that which has been sacrificed. Of course, Jesus did not mean that the man who leaves one house will receive many houses or 100 houses in return, but he did teach that the things sacrificed will be replaced manifold with the things which actually satisfy man's heart.

(3) *In Foretelling His Death and Resurrection, 18:31-34.* Jesus had earlier foretold His death (9:22,44; 13:33) and now in the concluding aspects of His journey toward Jerusalem reminds His disciples again that it is necessary for the Son of Man to suffer. Gradually He had enlarged their knowledge of His impending death until finally in this moment He states that His suffering and death are the purposes for this journey to the city. He even revealed the details of the suffering (vss. 32-33). His disciples, however, did not understand His teachings. They had pictured Jesus as a militant deliverer and at least two—James and John—were to seek places of prominence in an earthly kingdom. Now the Master speaks of subsequent sorrow, agony, and death. Luke explains (v. 34) their misunderstandings in three different modes of expression, but all of them simply suggest that the disciples could not understand the way of suffering and death. Only the resurrection experiences could bring understanding to them.

(4) *In Healing a Blind Man, 18:35-43.* As Jesus and His companions moved toward Jerusalem, they passed through Jericho for His last time. A blind beggar was seated by the highway and was begging from those who traveled this road. His keen ears were sensitive to the movement and noise of this crowd and he asked, "What does this mean?" The crowd replied, "Jesus of Nazareth is passing by." Having heard that Jesus passed by, the blind man addressed Him as Son of David (Messiah) and begged for pity. The crowd rebuked the blind man and insisted that he be quiet, but the man cried out more forcefully. Jesus stopped and ordered the blind man brought to Him. Standing near Jesus, the blind man again begged to receive his sight. Jesus said, "Receive your sight; your faith has made you whole." The man immediately received his sight and followed Jesus. All the people joined the blind man in praising God for Jesus' miracle.

The sovereignty of the Lord is also disclosed by the fact that Jesus permitted this man to address Him as Messiah. Previously He had refused to allow others to address Him publicly by this term (4:35,41; 9:21,36). This declaration of Messiahship by the blind man of Jericho anticipates the assertions of the triumphal entry (19:37-

40). However, the differences between His conception of Messiahship and theirs remained drastic.

(5) *In Visiting a Publican, 19:1-10.* Jericho was located on the main route from Trans-Jordan to Jerusalem; therefore, many tax collectors worked along this road to collect their customs. Zacchaeus headed the tax collections in this region and lived in Jericho, the logical site to collect the taxes on goods from Egypt to Jordan. His vocation excluded him from membership in the community of God's people. It is likely that Zacchaeus had previously heard of Jesus, the nonconformist who dared to socialize with Gentiles. Consequently, Zacchaeus ran ahead of the crowds and climbed into a sycamore tree to see Jesus. When Jesus came to Zacchaeus' vantage point, He looked into the tree and commanded the tax collector to descend. The expression states that Jesus must (*dei*, of moral necessity) abide in the publican's house. This man immediately descended from his place and happily began the journey which would take him and Jesus to the publican's house. The crowds murmured their criticisms, but Jesus was not deterred by their appraisal of His character.

This contact with Jesus impressed Zacchaeus, who declared that he would give half his goods to the poor and pledged to restore fourfold anything that had been taken in extortion. Jesus then observed that Zacchaeus had seen his guilt, had confessed his sin, and that salvation had come to the publican's house. That the publican was a descendant of Abraham is true, but his repentance made him a spiritual son of Abraham.

The sovereignty of the Lord has again been revealed in His willingness to oppose diametrically the Jewish social and religious customs. The account is concluded by the observation that His eternal purpose is seen in His seeking and saving the lost.

(6) *In Rewarding His Servants, 19:11-28.* Jesus spoke the parable of the pounds just a few days before the crucifixion. The parable was spoken prior to beginning the last journey along the winding road of 17 miles leading from Jericho up to the Holy City. These words were addressed primarily to His disciples and teach that all men who believe in Jesus have the opportunity to work in His kingdom. Those who use wisely their opportunities build us a treasure in heaven; those who neglect them become spiritual dwarfs.

Verse 11 gives the reason for the parable: He was near Jerusalem and His disciples believed mistakenly that the kingdom of God would immediately appear. The parable revolves around a certain nobleman, a man of influence and possessions, who was to leave his estate and journey into a distant land to receive a kingdom. The nobleman called his ten servants and made each responsible for a pound, indicating that they were to care for this pound until he returned (v. 13).

When the nobleman had accomplished the purpose of his visit to the foreign country, he returned to his estate and called his servants, commanding them to give an account of their stewardship. The first reported that he had gained ten pounds by using the pound his lord had entrusted to him. The nobleman replied, "Well, thou good servant: because thou hast been faithful in a very little, have thou authority over ten cities." The second man indicated that his stewardship had been responsible for gaining five additional pounds. The nobleman then made him responsible for five cities. The third man came and indicated that he had kept the pound, having carefully wrapped it in a napkin. He explained his action on the basis that the master was an austere man (rough to the taste, stringent) and that his harshness had often resulted in the unkind and unfair treatment of others. This explanation did not please the nobleman, who proceeded to judge his servant harshly. He indicated that the servant could have deposited the money in a bank and at least received interest. He then commanded that the pound be taken from the negligent servant and given to the individual who had ten pounds. Some of his subjects objected that the man already controlled ten pounds; the nobleman replied that to the one who possesses it shall be given, and from the one who has not, even that which he has shall be taken away.

This parable contains in embryonic form the law of spiritual life. The man who does not employ his spiritual gifts loses them; the man who employs them finds them multiplied.

For Further Study

1. Read John 4:1-42. Read the article entitled "Samaritan" in *The International Standard Bible Encyclopedia*, pp. 2673-2674. Does this explain the uniqueness of the Samaritan leper's gratitude?
2. Compare Luke 17:20-37, I Thessalonians 4:13-5:11, and II Thessalonians 2:1-17. Note particularly the emphasis upon the suddenness of the Lord's return.
3. The sovereignty of Jesus is a neglected doctrine. Compare Luke 18:15-19:28 and Colossians 1:13-22.
4. What is the contemporary basis for reward? How does it differ generally from Jesus' criterion? See Luke 19:11-28.

Part IV

Final Aspects of the Ministry

CHAPTER NINE

The Ministry in Jerusalem

Luke's account has now brought Jesus to the Holy City. However, the ministry of Jesus was not concluded with His entry into the city. Christendom would be much poorer apart from many of the precious teachings spoken during His Jerusalem ministry. This ministry continued to emphasize His authority, His forgiveness, and His approaching death.

1. *Sunday, 19:29-44.* The activities of Sunday establish the background for the last phase of Jesus' public ministry.

(1) *His Entry into the City, 19:29-40.* The prophet Zechariah (Zechariah 9:9) had spoken centuries earlier concerning the Messiah's entry into Jerusalem. The prophet described his entry as that of a prince of peace. Luke definitely presents the triumphal entry as a messianic act. When the messianic band arrived near the city (in the area of Bethphage and Bethany), the Saviour commissioned two of His disciples to enter the village of Bethphage where they would find a colt tied. The disciples found the colt just as Jesus had predicted, the owners questioned their action as the Lord had also indicated they would, but the disciples carefully followed Jesus' instructions in answering the owners.

Jesus probably awaited the return of the two disciples in a small village on the southeastern edge of the Mount of Olives. Upon returning to the village, the disciples placed their garments upon the animal, and Jesus rode him triumphantly into the city. Many people spread their clothes in the roadway. Others cried, "Blessed be the

King that cometh in the name of the Lord: peace in heaven, and glory in the highest." What a contrast between the entry of the Prince of Peace and some Roman dignitary!

The common people accepted Jesus and recognized His kingship, but the Pharisees insisted that Jesus rebuke His disciples for their erroneous statement concerning His kingship. Jesus declared that it was impossible for His followers to remain silent; if they should, then the stones of the ground would cry in His honor. Jesus' reply to the Pharisees (vss. 39-40) asserts that His entry was Messianic in character. Jesus' Messiahship was now publicly revealed just prior to His death. Israel stood at the crossroad. The Jew must accept or reject the Messiahship of Jesus!

(2) *His Weeping over the City, 19:41-44.* These verses describe the deep concern and chagrin of Jesus, who wept over the city. The term "wept" likely carries with it the idea of "bursting into tears." In passion and pity He recognized that "this was the day." Verses 43-44 foretell the destruction of the city which will come because of the hardness of the Jewish hearts. For three years they had refused to believe Jesus and to accept Him. Jesus knew that the Romans would eventually destroy the city, the total destruction betrayed in the words "shall lay thee even with the ground. . . ."

2. *Monday, 19:45-48.* The cleansing of the Temple is a fulfillment of the prophecy of Malachi 3:1, spoken centuries before concerning the coming of God's Messiah to the Holy Temple. Jesus had begun His public ministry by cleansing the Temple; He concluded His ministry in the same manner. It is necessary to compare the Marcan account (11:11 ff.) to obtain the chronological events of this period.

Many trafficked in the sale of sacrifices to those who had journeyed to Jerusalem. Initially this practice was solely for convenience, but in Jesus' day it was practiced for exorbitant financial profits. The synoptic parallels (Matthew 21:12 ff., Mark 11:11 ff.) complement Luke's account by suggesting some of the details involved in the cleansing of the Temple. Luke emphasizes the ritual aspect of this purification. Luke further adds that Jesus was teaching daily in the Temple, arousing the animosity and antagonism of the chief priests and scribes. Yet, Jesus' popularity prevented His enemies from arresting Him. The people were literally "hanging upon his words."

The purification and cleansing of the Temple suggests that Jesus remains the purifier of religious experience. Perfect in love and action, He could never look favorably upon the base commercial activity enacted in the Temple area in the name of religious service. He openly claimed authority in the Temple, God's house, thereby forcing His death. Jesus did not belong to a priestly lineage; His priesthood, according to the epistle to the Hebrews, is of divine origin. The cleansing of the Temple suggests that Jesus was unhappy and displeased with the routine events involved in the Jewish religion of His day.

3. *Tuesday, 20:1-22:6.* The Tuesday of Passion Week was an extremely busy day in the ministry of Jesus. The day was characterized by various interrogations of Jesus, by His questioning of the scribes, and by His subsequent condemnation of them and the Pharisees. Other activities included the commendation of the widow, the eschatological discourse, the prediction of His betrayal by Judas, and the prediction of His subsequent crucifixion.

(1) *Questions Directed to Jesus, 20:1-40.* The attempts of His enemies to ensnare Jesus are obvious in the series of questions addressed to Him.

a. *The Sanhedrin's Challenge of Jesus' Authority, 20:1-19.* Jesus' purification of the Temple was a dramatic and severe interference in Jewish religious life. Here was an impostor, who did not come from a priestly lineage or even a Levitical background, suggesting that He had authority over the highest ecclesiastical groups of His day. As a result of this, the Jewish Council sent representatives to interrogate Him at the point of His religious authority. By what authority did He achieve these things? Jesus answered their questions with a question concerning the baptism of John. Was John's baptism authorized by heaven, or by men? The representatives of the Sanhedrin easily followed Jesus' logic and reasoned that they could not answer, "From heaven." If so, Jesus would then ask, "Why did you not believe him?" On the other hand, the authorities reasoned that they could not answer, "Of men." If so, the people would stone them inasmuch as the masses believed John to have been a prophet. Jesus had so effectively defeated the Sanhedrin at its own game that its representatives simply replied that they could not tell the source of John's baptism. It was obvious to Jesus and to the people that the religious leaders denied the authority by which John had acted (cf. John 1:29 ff.).

This encounter with representatives of the Sanhedrin prompted Jesus to speak the parable of the wicked husbandmen. The man

planted a vineyard and gave its responsibilities to certain husbandmen. The owner then journeyed into a far country for an extended
period of time. At the end of the growing season, he sent a servant to
the husbandmen and requested his portion of the fruit from the
vineyard. However, the husbandmen beat the servant and sent him
away empty-handed. The owner sent another servant, but he was
likewise beaten by the husbandmen. The owner finally sent a third
servant, who was also wounded by the husbandmen. The lord of the
vineyard then decided to send his beloved son, believing that the
husbandmen would surely revere him because of his relationship to
the owner. Yet, the husbandmen had no respect for the son and
killed him, believing that the vineyard would then become theirs. But
the owner of the vineyard came and destroyed these husbandmen, in
turn giving the vineyard to others.

The point had been forcefully made. This parable elicited sympathy and sorrow from Jesus' hearers. Their sorrow prompted Jesus
to compare Himself to a stone rejected by the builders, but nevertheless a stone which became the cornerstone. Jesus recognized that
some would stumble at the stone; they would be broken. Others
would be crushed by the stone itself. The chief priest and scribes
obviously interpreted the parable as Jesus had intended and immediately sought to arrest Him, but they refrained because they feared the
multitudes.

The parable of the wicked husbandmen obviously was directed
toward the Jewish nation and her leaders. Many of God's prophets
had been beaten and rejected. As a last resort, He sent His own Son;
but the Jewish people elected to kill Him, thinking His death would
resolve all their problems.

b. *The Question of Tribute Money, 20:20-26.* The Jewish
leaders did not succeed in ensnaring Jesus in their interrogations of
His authority employed in the Temple, but this defeat did not stop
them in their attempt to execute Him. Verse 19 indicates that Jesus
maintained an unusual influence over the multitudes; the Jewish
leaders were reluctant to attempt His execution because of His popularity. The Sanhedrin then sent a number of their younger disciples
(Matthew 22:16 ff.) in an attempt to ensnare Him in His speech. The
aged and mature men of the Sanhedrin could never disguise their
hatred under the cloak of seeking answers to their questions, but the
younger men could pretend that they earnestly sought an answer to
their religious-political question. Their approach began in extreme
flattery (v. 21), but they hoped to conclude the conversation only

after having involved Jesus in a controversy with the policies of the Roman government. The Roman system of taxation was well-established, and the Jews despised both the system and the personalities in it. The question asked of Jesus, "Is it lawful for us to give tribute unto Caesar, or no?" was designed to create a dilemma to which there was no solution. If Jesus answered affirmatively and approved taxation, He would then incur the disfavor of the Jews. If He answered negatively and denied the well-established system of taxation, then in essence He would deny the authority of the Roman government and would incur the hatred of Rome.

He perceived their deed and requested a coin bearing Caesar's image. He asked whose image the coin bore, and the people replied the inscription was Caesar's. Jesus therefore concluded that one is to give to Caesar the things belonging to him and to give to God the things belonging to God. His answer was so straightforward and logical that the second plan devised by the Jewish leaders to ensnare Him was foiled (cf. 23:2).

This experience illustrates Jesus' recognition of governmental authority, but it also illustrates Jesus' conviction that man's relationship to God is of supreme significance.

c. *The Question of Resurrection, 20:27-40.* Many of the high priests were Sadducees, a Jewish religious party having its stronghold in the Temple and largely controlling the political life of the people. The Sadducees were closely related to the Roman government and seemed to be more interested in politics than in religion. The party was the antithesis of the Pharisees in almost every respect. The Sadducees disbelieved the doctrine of resurrection, and this conviction made their question even more hypocritical.

The question was based on the levirate (brother-in-law) law of marriage. Moses (Deuteronomy 25:5 ff.) gave this law in order to protect the childless wife. If brothers lived together and one died having no child, then one of his brothers should marry the brother's wife and the first-born son of the union would then bear the name of the deceased brother. They spoke of the woman's being married to seven brothers, but still she remained childless. Whose wife would she be in the resurrection?

Jesus' answer cuts through the hypocrisy and theoretical arrangement posed by the Sadducees, stating that the resurrection life will not be created in the conditions of the earthly life. The ordinary and routine activities of marital relationships cease; however, the future life is more drastically different from earthly existence than at

the point of marital relationship. In the future life men are described
as equal with angels and as being the children of God (v. 36). The
immortality of the future life explains why marital relationships are
not continued.

Jesus was not satisfied with this sharp repudiation of the theoretical question; He then turned to show the Sadducees that the Pen-
tateuch (the only portion of the Old Testament accepted by the
Sadducees) taught resurrection. Jesus referred to Moses' testimony at
the burning bush. On that occasion, Moses addressed God as the God
of Abraham, the God of Isaac, and the God of Jacob. The patriarchs
were immortal, otherwise God would never have been called the God
of the living, but rather the God of the dead. His relationship with
the patriarchs continued because they lived.

Jesus' answer to the Sadducees declares that there is a resurrection, that the resurrection relationships will not be re-created in the
image of earthly relationships, and that God is God of the living.

(2) *A Question Asked by Jesus, 20:41-44.* It was then time for
Jesus to pose a question. He directed His question to the Jews in an
attempt to assist them in effecting the proper relationship between the
Father and the Son. Luke has carefully indicated that the people
hated Jesus because of His claims to identification with God. Jesus
asked, "How say they that Christ is David's son?" He then chose
Psalm 110:1 as an answer to His own question. "The Lord said unto
my Lord, Sit thou on my right hand, Till I make thine enemies thy
footstool." David thereby declared the Messiah to be his descendant
(cf. II Samuel 7:8-29; Micah 5:2). Certain New Testament books
establish this relationship (cf. Matthew 1:1; Romans 1:3). Although
He is a ruler of the line of David, He is more than an earthly ruler.
Jesus claimed to be the Messiah of God. This claim of Jesus is a
claim to more than military leadership; it is a claim to lordship. The
question remains, "If David called him Lord, then how is he his
son?" This question can be answered only by placing the doctrines of
the inspiration of the scriptures, the humanity of the Messiah, and the
deity of Jesus in proper perspective.

(3) *The Condemnation of the Scribes and Pharisees, 20:45-47.*
The scribal office had probably originated during the Exile, but in
Jesus' day the scribes had come to be the legalistic and professional
interpreters of the law. Jesus delineated their hypocrisy by referring
to their personal desires: salutations in the market places, chief seats
in the synagogues, chief places at feasts, and long flowing robes. The
honors which they desired were extraordinary. Their office was

marked by the clothing they wore; their person by the salutations they received. To address the scribe as "Master" or "My Master" was imperative. The scribes even claimed to rank above their parents and always arranged for descending rank of evaluation within their group. They wished to occupy the chief seats (those facing the people) in the synagogues and the chief places (to the right and left of the host respectively in descending order of importance) at feasts. Yet, these people who were so externally correct were inwardly corrupt. Jesus' solemn pronouncement is that these shall receive greater condemnation.

Again Jesus emphasizes the qualities of true internal religious experience in opposition to external exaggerations which have nothing to do with the purity and cleanness of heart.

(4) *The Commendation of the Widow, 21:1-4.* The scene revealed in these verses is one of tenderness and understanding. Having silenced His opponents with answers which they were unable to refute, Jesus looked up from His seat over against the treasury and observed a widow placing her gifts into the Temple treasury. The treasury was located in the Court of the Women and consisted of some 13 trumpet-shaped collection boxes, narrow at the top and wider at the base. The gift made by the widow was indeed small, consisting of two mites. In contemporary parlance one might suggest that Jesus observed the widow offering a gift of less than a penny. However, her gift was greater than all others because gifts are measured not by what one gives but rather by what remains after he has given. The rich people had given of their abundance; she had given all her possessions. Faith must have prompted this sacrificial gift.

Jesus' observation concerning this small gift has likely inspired larger gifts than anything which any man has ever said or done. The spirit of trust prompted her to give all that she had. It is that spirit which leads an individual to commit himself totally and unselfishly to the Messiah.

(5) *The Eschatological Discourse, 21:5-38.* This eschatological section is divided into two parts: the destruction of Jerusalem and the coming of the Son of Man:

a. *The Destruction of Jerusalem, 21:5-24.* The Jews were unusually proud of the Temple edifice. Some of the people spoke of its unique adornment and its great wealth guaranteed by its religious sacrifices and offerings. In this discourse, occasioned by their reference to the Temple, Jesus declared that the leaders, the city, and even the great Temple were doomed to destruction. Solomon had built the first Temple approximately 1,000 years prior to Jesus' time, and a Temple with its sacrificial and offering system had existed (except during the Babylonian Exile) since that time. For approximately 1,000 years, with the exception of the previously-mentioned Babylonian captivity (and some three years during the reign of Antiochus Epiphanes, 168-165 B.C.), the Temple had remained as the focal point of Jewish life. Elements of fraud and deception had entered into the Temple ceremonies and practices, but still it had remained as the great institution of Judaism. Although the Temple had been regarded as one of the great wonders of the ancient world, Jesus predicted that the Temple would be completely destroyed, not even one stone being left upon another (v. 6). Such a graphic description of the destruction created additional curiosity in the hearts of His hearers, who inquired concerning the time of this event and the signs preceding it (v. 7). False messiahs would appear prior to the Lord's return (parousia), but their appearance was not to deceive His followers. His disciples were also to understand that the world would be characterized by war and turmoil, but these characteristics were not to deter a faith in the imminent return of the Lord. Famine and pestilence (v. 11) were also to prevail prior to the Lord's return. Even more personal and intimate was the prediction that the disciples themselves would be persecuted (v. 12). Although the disciples would be betrayed by their relatives and closest friends, Jesus promised protection (v. 18). Nothing outside the will of God could occur to them. The disciples were to persevere in their faith and thereby were to maintain control under the most difficult extenuating circumstances (v. 19).

Jesus then turned to discuss the signs relative to the destruction of Jerusalem (vss. 20-24). Jerusalem was to be surrounded by armies; the presence of the armies indicated that the time of destruction was near. These would be terrible days of persecution, but His disciples were to remember that all these events fulfilled prophecy (v. 22). The terribleness of retribution would even reach the blessed experience of motherhood in these days. Motherhood would be a curse instead of a blessing (v. 23). The Jewish defenders of the city would fall by the sword, and those who were not killed would be taken captive. The Holy City, now standing in all its grandeur and glory, would be trodden down by the Gentiles "until the times of the Gentiles be fulfilled" (v. 24). This expression, "the times of the Gentiles," seems to refer to the period between the destruction of the city and the second coming of Christ.

The prophecy relative to the destruction of the city was fulfilled in A.D. 70, when Titus led a Roman army against the city. After a siege of five months the Romans overthrew the city and plundered and destroyed the Temple, slaying thousands of Jewish men, women, and children. Mothers were made prisoners of war and not one Jew was left alive in the city of Jerusalem. For years, no Jew was allowed to enter the region of Jerusalem. On the anniversary of Jerusalem's devastation the Jews were permitted to go to the hills and mourn their city's destruction.

b. *The Parousia of the Messiah, 21:25-38.* This portion of the prophetic discourse relates solely to those events relative to the return of the Son of Man. In Jesus' brief record concerning the parousia, He suggested a number of miraculous signs to precede the end of the age. Employing typical Jewish terminology, Jesus spoke in terms of cosmic upheaval to occur in the elements of nature. These phenomena will frighten Jesus' adversaries, but His disciples will realize that their final redemption is near.

Jesus at this time chose to illustrate spiritual truth in parabolic form. Selecting the fig tree as His illustration, He suggested that the appearance of buds warned of approaching summer. Even so the appearance of the strange physical phenomena warns of the imminency of Jesus' return. His generation was not to pass away until all these things should be accomplished (v. 32). This difficult verse has been interpreted as a reference to numerous historical events: the crucifixion, the resurrection, the destruction of the city, and so forth. It seems that Jesus was obviously referring to the destruction of Jerusalem. Many of His generation would have been alive in A.D. 70, and would have witnessed the fulfillment of His prophecy.

The components of this discourse are extremely difficult to separate. The division offered is one which seems to be logical, although as has been admitted, verse 32 likely refers to the destruction of the city. The emphasis of the entire discourse is the fact that Jesus is Lord of history and therefore dominates the world scene regardless of external circumstances.

Verses 34-36 serve as a solemn warning against spiritual lethargy. One is to be alert spiritually lest his heart be replete with debauchery, drunkenness, worldliness, and anxiety, and thereby fail to recognize the approach of the end of the age. The parousia affects not only the Jewish nation, but also the whole world. Therefore, the people are to watch (be sleepless) and be alert for every sign fulfilling Jesus' warning.

Verses 37-38 relate again Jesus' activities during Passion Week —teaching in the Temple during the day and spending the nights outside Jerusalem. His popularity continued regardless of the repeated attacks by the Jewish religious leaders.

(6) *The Predictions of the Betrayal by Judas and Jesus' Subsequent Crucifixion, 22:1-6.* Jesus had come to Jerusalem for the annual observance of the Passover. The Passover was one of the Mosaic feasts and had been instituted at the time of the passing of the death angel (see Exodus 12). Luke also refers to the Feast of Unleavened Bread, which technically began on the night of the Passover and continued for seven days. The two feasts were popularly referred to as the Passover. Jews from throughout the world came to Jerusalem for the observance of this feast. Although the chief priests and scribes were seeking some method of arresting and executing Jesus, they were continually fearing the people.

Satan entered into Judas Iscariot, who went to the chief priests and captains of the Temple to effect a bargain whereby Jesus could be delivered. One of His own became the means of delivering Jesus apart from a riot or insurrection by the common people. Luke discloses that the chief priests were willing to give him money; Matthew (26:15) identifies the money as 30 pieces of silver. The bargain was sealed: Judas promised to betray Jesus when the multitudes were absent. The inflammatory social circumstances of the Passover were further endangered by the activity of the Zealots, extremists who felt that the dagger was the choicest way to deal with their enemies.

The records do not indicate that Judas was forced to betray Jesus; there is every evidence to the contrary. In the light of Judas' decision the Jewish leaders no longer needed to plot against Jesus and plan His arrest.

4. *Thursday, 22:7-53.* Tuesday had been a busy day filled with discourse including interrogation and discussion, as well as routine teaching ministries. Wednesday's activities are unrecorded, but the day was likely spent in the quiet companionship of His disciples. Thursday began another day of activity confined essentially to the apostolic circle and culminating in Jesus' arrest.

(1) *Preparation for the Passover, 22:7-13.* The people began preparation on the night before the Passover, that is, the evening

following the thirteenth of Nisan. It was necessary for the householders to search their houses thoroughly, collect all the leaven, and burn it on the following day. By noon on the fourteenth of Nisan, the leaven was to have been destroyed and the unleavened bread made ready for the Passover. The paschal lambs were slaughtered between 2:30 P.M. and 6:00 P.M. on the fourteenth of Nisan. A perfect lamb was slain by its owner, its blood caught in a Temple vessel and then passed along a line of priests until it was dashed upon the altar. In this sense, each worshiper sacrificed his own Passover offering.

Jesus selected two of His most trusted disciples, Peter and John, to prepare for the feast. He indicated (v. 10) that upon entering the city a man bearing a pitcher of water would meet them. They were to follow him into the house he entered and say to the owner, "The Master saith unto thee, where is the guest chamber, where I shall eat the Passover with my disciples?" Jesus further instructed that this man would show them a large, furnished upper room where they were to make their preparations.

The secrecy surrounding the preparation for the Passover is best explained on the basis that Jesus desired to eat this Passover with His disciples; therefore, Judas was frustrated in any attempt to deliver Jesus prematurely. The disciples would have no difficulty in selecting the man to follow; a water pitcher he carried would be a distinguishing mark. In Palestine only women customarily carried pitchers of water.

(2) *The Passover Meal, 22:14-34.* Jesus seemingly journeyed later in the day to the house where the preparations for the Passover had been made. Judas had no earlier opportunity to inform the Jewish authorities concerning Jesus' movements. Luke does not give an extensive account of the institution of the Lord's Supper, but simply records that Jesus desired "with desire" to partake of the Passover with His disciples prior to His suffering. Jesus informed His disciples that He would not eat the Passover again until He observed it with them in the kingdom of God. Many interpreters suggest that Jesus refers to the Passover as symbolizing a messianic banquet. The cup to which Luke refers (v. 17) is one of the four cups drunk during the Passover meal. It logically seems as if this was the cup drunk immediately prior to the introduction of the Passover itself. Jesus again indicated that this was His last observance with His disciples until the consummation of the age (v. 18).

The formal introduction of the Lord's Supper is briefly stated by Luke (vss. 19-20). Jesus took the unleavened bread, broke it and handed it to His disciples, saying, "This is my body which is given for you: this do in remembrance of me." The broken bread serves as a symbol of a body broken in sacrificial death. The statement of Jesus, "This do in remembrance of me," suggests the nature and purpose of the Supper. The Supper symbolizes the sacrifice of Jesus and in no fashion carries with it sacramental significance. He also took the cup and said, "This cup is the new testament in my blood, which is shed for you." The blood is the new covenant in which His people are related to Him. The sacrificial aspect of His approaching death is underscored in the words "which is shed for you."

Verses 21-23 reminded His followers that His betrayer was at the table. However, Jesus wished them to understand that Judas was totally responsible for his action and that Jesus' sacrificial death was in keeping with God's eternal purpose. The disciples did not comprehend and began to question one another concerning the meaning of the Master's words (v. 23).

Even in the midst of Jesus' suffering and agony, His disciples could not be satisfied with their own personal positions in the kingdom and argued concerning which one was the greatest. Jesus (v. 25) reminded them that this discussion was after the character of the Gentiles who exercise lordship over their subjects. He redefined the meaning of greatness, suggesting that the man who is truly great spiritually does not desire to make his contemporaries know his importance—rather, he wishes to be of service to all. In the Jewish society of Jesus' day the superior man was served by the inferior, and yet the eternal Son of God appeared among His people as a servant. Jesus reprimanded the disciples for their selfish ambitions, reminding them (vss. 28-29) that they had lived with Him during His temptations and should have been fully aware of the problems which He had confronted. He promised them a position of greatness in the eternal kingdom, a position in which they are to eat and drink at His table and to occupy places of judgment. These thrones of judgment are relative to the tribes of Israel. Therefore, the disciples were not to anticipate earthly position and worldly power, but a heavenly joy and honor in His eternal kingdom. The disciples had observed the trials and temptations of Jesus; surely they would not expect to be exempt from similar problems. Jesus had appointed for them a kingdom even as the Father had appointed a kingdom for Him.

On the same evening Jesus reminded Simon (Peter) of Satan's intent to try him. Jesus did not call Simon by the term "Peter" (rock). He addressed him as Simon, referring to the disciple as an ordinary man, frail and weak. The omniscience of Jesus is evidenced by His prayer for Peter that God's power would sustain him. Jesus spoke of Peter's fall (v. 32) and commanded him to strengthen his fellow disciples once he had turned back to the Lord. Peter avowed his willingness both to go to prison and to death for the sake of the Saviour. But Jesus reminded Peter that the cock would not crow before Peter had denied his Master three times!

(3) *The Last Teaching, 22:35-38.* Jesus had twice commissioned His disciples and had sent them on the missions without materialistic possessions, insisting at the time that they depend entirely upon God (9:3; 10:4). He reminded them of His previous exhortations and then asked, "Did you lack anything?" They replied that they lacked nothing and that God's provision had been more than adequate. However, Jesus predicted that following His crucifixion the disciples should take whatever materialistic possessions they had. With the crucifixion of the Lord and the spreading of persecution against the Christians, the disciples could well expect additional discrimination and difficulty. Jesus instructed the disciple who had no sword to sell his garments and buy one.

Jesus was to be numbered among the transgressors, and the physical suffering which He was to endure would later be directed toward His followers. Jesus did not mean for the disciples literally to sell their garments and purchase swords. He was suggesting to them that their lives would be subjected to swords, not love. Their battle would not be one of a sword and spear, but a battle of the spirit (Ephesians 6:17).

(4) *The Gethsemane Prayer, 22:39-46.* A favorite place for the Master to pray was Gethsemane (v. 39), a site on the Mount of Olives. His disciples followed Him to the garden, which Luke describes as "the place." Jesus withdrew a few yards from the group and knelt to pray. His prayer reveals an honest and sincere searching of His heart in relationship to the will of God. If the Father willed to remove the cup of suffering, then Jesus begged for this; if the Father willed that He should drink the cup, then He was ready to accept the Father's will. Verse 42 is an epitome of total commitment to an eternal purpose.

Although Jesus was removed from the disciples about the distance of a stone's cast, He was not separated from God. An angel appeared from heaven and strengthened Him. The Saviour continued agonizing concerning the eternal will and prayed the more earnestly so that the tissues of His body broke—His perspiration was as great drops of blood falling to the ground. When He had finished His prayer, He returned to His sleeping disciples and asked, "Why sleep ye? Rise and pray, lest ye enter into temptation." Jesus had agonized in prayer while His disciples had slept. Is it possible that today no one cares enough to watch?

(5) *The Betrayal and Arrest, 22:47-53.* Judas had led a group composed of Temple guards and members of the Sanhedrin to the garden for the purpose of arresting Jesus. Judas stepped forward and with a kiss identified the Lord. Jesus was not helpless in this moment, and some of His followers asked if they should attack with a sword. In fact, Peter did cut off the ear of Malchus, the servant of the high priest (John 18:10). Jesus quickly healed Malchus' ear. His kindness was further accented by His questioning of the attitudes of those who came to arrest Him as a thief (v. 52). When Jesus taught in the Temple, the guards made no attempt to arrest Him. If Jesus had been guilty of their accusations and they had been interested in following the avenues of justice, they would have arrested Him earlier. His captors did not work simply under the cover of night. They also worked in the power of evil.

FOR FURTHER STUDY

1. Read Alfred Edersheim's *The Temple*, p. 35-81, or Edersheim's *The Life and Times of Jesus the Messiah*, Vol. 1, pp. 243 ff., 369-372, for a description of the Temple courts and activities.

2. Describe the shrewdness of Jesus in answering the question concerning tribute money. What made the question so potentially dangerous?

3. Compare Luke 21:5-36 with Mark 13 and Matthew 24-25.

4. Read H. E. Dana's *The New Testament World*, p. 114, for a description of the Passover.

5. What elements constituted the Passover feast?

6. See the article "Mount of Olives" in *The International Standard Bible Encyclopedia*, pp. 2185-2190, for an excellent description of the mountain. Why did Jesus retire there to pray? Why were gardens outside the city walls?

CHAPTER TEN

The Crucifixion and Resurrection

The concluding verses of Luke's gospel move with great rapidity from one historical event to another, detailing events preceding His trial, the crucifixion scene, the resurrection, and finally the appearances and ascension of the Master.

1. *Friday, 22:54-23:56.* Jesus was arrested on Thursday evening, which was actually during the early hours of the Jewish Friday; the Jewish day began at 6:00 P.M. the previous evening. The following hours were filled with trials, mockeries, and rebukings. Not only did His enemies ridicule Him, one of His own disciples denied Him.

(1) *Peter's Denial, 22:54-65.* Peter's desire to follow Jesus into the house of the high priest revealed his loyalty. Peter was admitted into the inner court, where he joined the soldiers and other servants seated around the fire. The maid apparently became suspicious of Peter and surmised that he was a disciple of Jesus. She remarked to those gathered around the fire that Peter had been with Jesus. Peter, however, denied the accusation. A brief time later, still another servant identified him as one of the apostolic band. A second time Peter denied the accusation. After another hour had elapsed, another bystander confidently asserted that Peter had been with Jesus, for his Galilean speech had betrayed him. Again Peter denied the accusation, and while he was speaking the cock crowed. The Lord then turned and looked at Peter (v. 61), who remembered the prediction of Jesus that he would deny his Master three times before the cock crowed. Peter's remorse and sorrow were revealed in the weeping of bitter tears.

(2) *Jesus' Trial Before the Sanhedrin, 22:66-71.* Jesus was tried six times. Three trials were religious: one before Annas, the former

high priest; one before Caiaphas and the Sanhedrin; and one early in the morning when He was formally condemned by the Sanhedrin. Three trials were civil: the first trial before Pilate; the interrogation by Herod; and the second trial before Pilate. Luke does not record the first religious trials, but he does mention the physical abuse (vss. 63-65) rendered Jesus by the religious people of His day. Inasmuch as the sentence of death could not be legally passed during the night, the Sanhedrin reconvened early in the morning for the purpose of condemning Him to death. This group had already made its decision concerning His future, but the Jews desperately needed some political basis on which to accuse Jesus. Thus they said, "If thou art the Christ, tell us." The Romans would readily execute one who appeared dangerous politically; they had no sincere interest in the religious problems about which the Jews constantly argued. If Jesus had given a simple affirmative answer to their question, then the Jews would have insisted that He was a political messiah of some nature. A simple negative answer would have been an untruth, for He was God's Messiah. Therefore, He replied, "If I tell you, you will not believe; and if I ask you, you will not answer." Jesus had already been prejudged and His answer would not have altered their contention. Jesus assured them, however, that their prejudice could not prevent His eternal association with God in power. He indicated that He would be seated at God's right hand, a place of authority and honor.

The mention of being seated at God's right hand provoked the Jews to ask still another question. "Art thou then the Son of God?" If Jesus admitted Sonship to God, then the Jews could charge Him with blasphemy. Pilate, the Roman governor, would not be swayed by His claim to deity, but the masses of the Jews would be prejudiced by such a claim. Jesus wisely answered the question in the words, "Ye say that I am." The Sanhedrin affirmed His Sonship; Jesus did not deny it. This admission stirred the Sanhedrin to claim that Jesus was guilty of blasphemy. They saw no need to proceed with the trial (v. 71), having heard His own testimony concerning Sonship.

(3) *Jesus' First Examination by Pilate, 23:1-7.* The Sanhedrin had previously condemned Jesus to death (22:66-71), but they now depended upon the Roman officials to enact the verdict. Jesus' trials included three before Roman rulers: two before Pilate, and one before Herod. The first appearance before Pilate occurred immediately following the Sanhedrin's formal condemnation of Jesus. Luke earlier indicated that the Jewish leaders feared the people (20:19) and

sought to camouflage their activities leading to the crucifixion. This explains their haste in pressuring Pilate and clamoring for the crucifixion (Mark 15:25).

Luke states that the entire multitude—Sadducees, Pharisees, scribes, and other groups which hated one another—appeared before Pilate. They continued to bring charges against Jesus, suggesting that He perverted the people (brought insurrection to their country), prohibited the paying of taxes to Caesar, and claimed to be their king. None of these charges were true. Pilate announced to the people that he found no fault in Jesus. His verdict was simple: Not guilty.

But this verdict did not satisfy the Jews, who the more vigorously claimed that Jesus was an insurrectionist (v. 5). Because of their claim that Jesus had created insurrection throughout all the Jewish lands, Pilate saw an opportunity to evade the responsibility of passing final judgment. Upon learning that Jesus was from Galilee, he sent him to Herod Antipas, the puppet king of Galilee, who had come to Jerusalem for the Passover festivities. Though convinced that Jesus was innocent, Pilate wished to maintain a good relationship with the Jews as well as with Tiberius Caesar, the Roman emperor. If Herod chose to judge Jesus as one of his own subjects, then Pilate would be released from all responsibility, both to the Jews and to Caesar.

(4). *Jesus' Appearance Before Herod, 23:8-12.* Herod was happy to have the privilege of meeting Jesus (v. 8). He had long wished to see Him because of the many reports he had heard of the Lord's activities. Most of all, he had wished to see some miracle performed by Jesus. Luke does not give the details of Herod's inquisition; the author scarcely mentions Jesus' silence during the extended interrogation. The chief priests and scribes who had accompanied Jesus to Herod's palace accused Him vehemently. Herod and his soldiers then treated Him with contempt, mocking Him and placing a counterfeit robe of royalty about His body.

The breach existing between Pilate and Herod was somewhat healed that day (v. 12) by Pilate's astute political decision. Having finished the mockery and contemptuous acts, Herod returned Jesus to Pilate.

(5) *Jesus' Second Trial Before Pilate, 23:13-25.* Now Pilate was again confronted by an innocent man subjected to the continued and false accusations of the Jewish leaders. Pilate reminded the Jews that he had pronounced the verdict: "Not guilty." He also reminded them that Herod had joined in his appraisal of their victim. Pilate proposed to chastise Jesus and then release Him—the governor had customari-

ly released one criminal at the time of the feast. Confronted with a
choice between Jesus and Barabbas, a noted murderer and insurrectionist, the people chose Barabbas. A second time Pilate attempted to
secure the release of Jesus, but the multitudes cried, "Crucify him,
crucify him!" A third time Pilate attempted to release Jesus by
asking, "Why, what evil hath he done?" The governor suggested
again that He be chastised and freed. Instantaneously the mob clam-
ored that Jesus be crucified. Ignoring the plea of his wife (Matthew
27:19) and the clamoring of his own conscience, Pilate sentenced
Jesus to crucifixion. Pilate released a murderer and insurrectionist,
but delivered Jesus to the will of the Jews.

(6) *Events Preceding the Crucifixion, 23:26-31.* Luke omits the
events which immediately followed the sentencing of Jesus and continues the narrative with the enlistment of Simon, a Cyrenian, to bear
the Saviour's cross. Jesus had borne His cross from Pilate's residence,
and when He faltered, the Roman soldiers drafted Simon to bear the
cross to Golgotha. Jesus' body had been torn by the heavy Roman
lash, a whip comparable to a cat-o'-nine-tails with bits of metal in the
ends of the lash. He was physically and emotionally exhausted from
the events of the preceding hours.

A number of people followed Jesus, the other two prisoners (v.
32), and their captors to the site of crucifixion. Included in the
number were some sympathetic women who cried aloud because of
Jesus' fate. In the midst of His torture and suffering, Jesus said to the
women, "Daughters of Jerusalem, weep not for me, but weep for
yourselves, and for your children." These words, along with those of
vss. 29-31, suggest the terrible suffering which was to come upon
Jerusalem. Certain interpreters believe the words, "For if they do
these things in a green tree, what shall be done in the dry?" to be a
popular proverb. Others associate the words with Proverbs 11:31,
Jeremiah 25:29, and Ezekiel 20:47. Perhaps the meaning is this: If
they do these terrible things to a green tree (Jesus), what shall they do
to the dry (Jews)? God's judgments were to fall upon all men. It was
unreasonable to use green wood for a fire; it was also unreasonable to
think of the Messiah's being subjected to these judgments.

(7) *The Crucifixion, 23:32-49.* Two other criminals were sentenced to be crucified at this time. The site of crucifixion was Calvary
(the Latin term) or Golgotha (the Hebrew term). After arriving at the
place of execution, the victim's body was placed upon a T-shaped
cross. His arms were extended and his hands were attached to the
upper crossbar by nails; his feet were lashed to the lower portion of

the cross. The cross was then lifted and its lower end was placed in a hole prepared for it.

While hanging on the cross, Jesus spoke seven times. His first words were, "Father, forgive them; for they know not what they do." These words reflect His grace and kindness. The soldiers charged with the crucifixion had the right to divide the victim's earthly possessions. The possessions were divided into four parts inasmuch as four soldiers, supervised by a centurion, were in charge of the execution. The coat, the long garment worn next to the skin, was seamless and may have been a valuable garment. In any case, the soldiers decided not to tear it, but to cast lots to determine who would receive it.

But Jesus not only suffered physically, He also suffered mentally. Luke recorded the taunting of the Jewish leaders who said, "He saved others; let him save himself, if he be Christ. . . ." For one time the leaders of the Jews spoke truth, although they did not recognize it as such. Jesus could not have saved Himself and also have become the Saviour of the world. Mark further indicates (15:29-30) that passers-by laughed and jeered. The soldiers also mocked Jesus and offered Him vinegar to quench His thirst. Their words had political connotations: "If thou be the King of the Jews, save thyself."

The Romans customarily placed a superscription on the cross noting the crime of the victim. The board placed on Jesus' cross contained the writing, "This is the King of the Jews." The superscription was written in Greek (language of philosophy and literature), Latin (language of law), and Hebrew (language of worship). Thus, all the people who watched the spectacle could know and understand the nature of His crime. Even in the superscription, Pilate's contempt of the Jew is readily seen. John records that the chief priest begged Pilate to change the wording to: "He said I am King of the Jews." Pilate dogmatically retained his previous notation (John 19:21-22).

One of the criminals treated Jesus contemptuously, saying, "If thou be Christ, save thyself and us." The other criminal rebuked his partner and asked, "Dost not thou fear God, seeing thou art in the same condemnation?" The second criminal recognized the justice of crucifixion as punishment for his crime; yet, he recognized the injustice of Jesus' crucifixion and declared that the Saviour had done nothing amiss. The second criminal then turned to Jesus and begged to be remembered whenever the Lord entered His kingdom (v. 42). The penitent criminal, convicted of his guilt and need of salvation, joyfully accepted the redemptive words of Jesus, "Verily I say unto thee, today shalt thou be with me in paradise." The criminal had begged for remembrance; he received a promise of fellowship in an eternal kingdom that same day. Jesus' promise was not one projected to the parousia; He dealt with the immediate future and indicated that the two would be together in paradise that day. The term *paradise* means "a garden place, a place of beauty and repose."

Jesus was crucified at approximately 9:00 A.M. and died at approximately 3:00 P.M. Verse 44 passes over the events from 12:00 P.M. to 3:00 P.M., indicating only that a great darkness covered all the earth. The true meaning of Jesus' sacrifice is explained in the simple words of v. 45, "The veil of the Temple was rent in the midst." Only one time during the year, on the Day of Atonement, did the high priest enter the Holy of Holies. Now the heavy veil of the Temple was split, signifying that the perfect sacrificial lamb makes possible the entry of every believer into the closest and most intimate fellowship with the Father. Luke's final record of Jesus' words from the cross is continued in v. 46: "Father, into thy hands I commend my spirit . . ." (Compare John 19:26-27, Mark 15:34, John 19:28, and John 19:30 for additional references to His words during the hours of crucifixion.) The hardened Roman captain had unquestionably witnessed many crucifixions. After having evaluated carefully all that he had seen and heard, he postulated that Jesus was a righteous man. He knew Jesus to be more than an ordinary man; by his words the centurion glorified God. The multitude who had observed the crucifixion were tremendously impressed with what they had seen and smote their breasts in guilt. The earthquake which accompanied the tearing of the Temple veil is not mentioned by Luke, but is recorded by Matthew (27:51-52).

The cross remains the focal point of all history. To Christendom it stands as an objective reality of God's love to a lost world. Its physical horribleness and agony must never overshadow its spiritual meaning.

(8) *The Burial of Jesus, 23:50-56.* Luke's record of Jesus' entombment is relatively brief in comparison with the account of the crucifixion. He does reveal that the Jews were anxious to bury the body because of the approaching Sabbath (v. 54). The credit for Jesus' burial is given to Joseph, further described as a counselor, a good and just man. Matthew (27:57) identifies Joseph of Arimathea as a secret follower of Jesus and a wealthy, distinguished member of the Sanhedrin. Luke also states that Joseph did not agree with the Sanhedrin's decision to ask for the Saviour's crucifixion. Joseph

risked persecution by the Jews in requesting the permission of Pilate
to bury the body of Jesus.

The tenderness of the scene is described in v. 53. Joseph, joined
by Nicodemus (John 19:39), took the body from the cross, wrapped
it in linen, and placed it in a sepulchre, which according to Matthew
(27:60) had been prepared for Joseph himself. John (19:39) indicates that the body of Jesus was anointed with an abundance of spices
(myrrh and aloes).

Jesus died at 3:00 P.M., and because the Sabbath began at
approximately 6:00 P.M. the Jews were anxious to bury the body
immediately so that the Sabbath would not be profaned. The author
describes the day as the "preparation" (v. 54), a technical Jewish
term to describe the day preceding the Sabbath. The women from
Galilee had faithfully followed Jesus and accompanied Joseph and
Nicodemus to the sepulchre. Then they returned to Jerusalem to
prepare spices and ointments to be used in anointing Jesus' body after
the Sabbath had ended.

2. *Sunday, 24:1-43*. The events of Sunday gave meaning to the
words of Paul in I Corinthians 15:17, "And if Christ be not raised,
your faith is vain; you are yet in your sins." Jesus had earlier spoken
of His passion and resurrection; the disciples had misunderstood His
words concerning the resurrection. This chapter portrays Jesus as the
Lord of death, as well as the Lord of life.

All the gospel writers join Luke in giving detailed accounts of
Jesus' activity following His resurrection. Yet not one of the writers
attempts to describe the resurrection. Human eyes did not witness the
scene. Nor do the gospel writers attempt any description of the
resurrection body of our Lord. It was not a material body of flesh,
resuscitated to a new physical existence as was that of Lazarus (John
11). Jesus' resurrection body was not subjected to the natural laws as
man understands them; He was able to appear or disappear at will,
even to the point of entering a room through a closed door. The
resurrection body is not to be understood simply as spirit. Jesus
invited Thomas to feel the nail prints and the scars left by the cross
experience and also ate in the presence of His disciples (Luke
24:37-43).

(1) *The Women Visit the Tomb, 24:1-11*. Luke carefully identifies the time of the women's visit to the tomb as being early dawn
on the first day of the week. The "first day" began at approximately
6:00 P.M. the previous evening. Upon reaching the tomb, they found
that the stone had been removed from the door. Mark (16:3) indi-

cates that the moving of the stone had constituted one of the problems discussed by the women while traveling to the tomb.

The women were surprised and frightened by the appearance of two men in dazzling apparel. Matthew (28:5) mentions an angel who spoke to the women. These two men in Luke's account are to be understood as angels; their message to the women is essentially the same as that of the angel of Matthew 28. "Why seek you the living among the dead? He is not here, but is risen. . . ." Jesus was resurrected and the tomb left empty!

The angel then reminded the women of Jesus' predictions of the crucifixion and resurrection (vss. 6-7). The women should have remembered the words of Jesus and therefore should not have come with spices to anoint a dead body. Luke (18:34) reveals that people did not understand His words relative to death and resurrection. He had spoken specifically of being raised on the third day; although they remembered His words, the words had not been accurately interpreted.

The women returned to the city, where they related their experiences. Luke (v. 10) identifies the women as Mary Magdalene, Joanna, and Mary the mother of James, along with some others unidentified. Although the women unquestionably substantiated one another's report, their words seemed as old wives' tales to those who refused to believe their testimonies.

(2) *The Visit of Peter to the Tomb, 24:12.* Peter ran to the sepulchre and found the tomb empty just as the women had described it. John 20:2 indicates that Peter was accompanied by John. The words describing Peter's activity at the sepulchre disclose that he stooped and peered into the empty tomb. He saw only the linen clothes laid by themselves. The empty tomb stood as an attestation to the women's testimonies, but still Peter was not able to comprehend what had occurred.

(3) *The Emmaus Experience, 24:13-35.* The first appearance mentioned by Luke is described extensively. The account concerns two men who were traveling the road to Emmaus, a village of some threescore furlongs (six or seven miles) from Jerusalem. Luke does not identify the two men; obviously they were not of the apostolic group, but two of Jesus' disciples. It has been conjectured that they were natives of Emmaus and were returning home following their observance of the Passover and the Feast of Unleavened Bread.

They were enthralled in discussion of the recent events which had occurred in the city of Jerusalem—events prior to the crucifixion, the crucifixion itself, and now the difficulty and mystery surrounding the death of Jesus. These men were prevented (v. 16) from knowing Jesus fully. Joining Himself to their company, Jesus inquired concerning the nature of their conversation.

Cleopas answered Jesus' question. His identity is uncertain, although some believe him to have been the brother of Joseph (Mary's husband). He interestingly answered the Master's question by replying with a question: "Art thou only a stranger in Jerusalem, and hast not known the things which have come to pass there in these days?" Jesus responded by asking for a more complete definition of the "things." The two ascribed the death of Jesus to the chief priests and rulers. The rulers of the Jews delivered Jesus to Pilate for the purpose of execution. The genuine disappointment of these men is registered in v. 21: "But we *trusted* that it had been he that should have redeemed *Israel* . . ." These men believed the past to be fulfilled in Jesus; the future they had committed to Him. But alas, this was the third day and Jesus had not appeared to them! They further recounted the experiences of the women who visited the tomb, which was found open and empty. The experience of Peter and John was also alluded to (v. 24), and again there was the suggestion that the sepulchre was empty even as the women had declared.

The dullness of the men prompted Jesus to guide the conversation. He rebuked them for their insensitivity to spiritual things (v. 25) and reminded them that it was morally necessary (*dei*) for Him to suffer these things. In a typical Jewish manner, Jesus began with the writings of Moses and continued with the prophets to explain the fulfillment of the scriptures in the life of the Messiah. This consumed time, and soon the three arrived near Emmaus. Jesus made as if to travel farther, but the two disciples compelled Him to abide there because of the late hour. During the evening meal, Jesus took bread, blessed it, broke it, and gave to them. Then their eyes were opened and they knew Him, that is, they fully recognized Him. Jesus then vanished. He would no longer be permanently with His disciples as He was prior to the crucifixion.

This revelation of Jesus' identity and His application of the scriptures to His own Messiahship caused the disciples' hearts to burn within them. The recent discovery made it impossible for them to remain in Emmaus; they immediately returned to Jerusalem, finding the apostolic band and relating to them what had occurred. "The Lord is risen indeed, and hath appeared to Simon" similarly constituted the testimony of the Jerusalem band to the two men from

Emmaus. The resurrection partially remained a mystery to both groups, but the certainty of the resurrection had been established.

(4) *Jesus' Appearance in Jerusaelm, 24:36-43*. Unquestionably this appearance is the same as recorded by John (20:19-25). Luke gives multiplied evidences for the resurrection of the Saviour. Prior to this time, Jesus had appeared only to small groups, or perhaps to individuals. Now He appeared to the entire group that all might know the truth of His resurrection. John complements Luke's account and indicates that the disciples had assembled in this place, likely the site of the Passover meal, because they feared the Jews.

On this Sunday evening, the disciples continued to struggle with the realities of Jesus' resurrection. Their hearts were filled with mingled feelings of fear, confidence, despair, and expectation. John states that the doors were closed (20:19), but Jesus suddenly appeared in their midst. His first words were, "Peace be unto you." Luke explains that they believed Him to be a spirit. To allay their fears and distress, He invited them to behold His hands and feet. They were further invited to touch His body and see that He was not a spirit. Jesus stood in spirit and in body, a glorified body and one very different from the human body. Paul describes the resurrection body in I Corinthians 15:35-58. Great joy overcame the disciples, who found it difficult to believe what they actually beheld. Noting their disbelief, Jesus asked for a piece of meat. The disciples then gave Him some meat and honeycomb which He ate.

3. *A Commission in Jerusalem, 24:44-49*. On this occasion (cf. Acts 1:3-8) the Master added that the messianic prophecies of Moses, the prophets, and Psalms were all fulfilled in His experience. These interpretations unlocked the disciples' understanding; they were then able to understand the Messiahship of Jesus in light of His crucifixion and resurrection. Jesus explained His suffering and agony as a part of God's eternal purpose (v. 46). God purposed this in order that repentance and remission of sins would be offered to all peoples (v. 47), beginning in Jerusalem. To begin in Jerusalem would indeed be strange to the Jew, who automatically thought of Jerusalem as being the Holy City—the city of the Great King and the center of Jewish religious activities.

Luke's account of this appearance concludes with Jesus' charge to His witnesses. He reminded them that they were witnesses of "these things" (crucifixion, resurrection, offering of repentance and remission of sin to all nations). They were to repeat the story of

God's eternal purpose as fulfilled in the person of His Son. Jesus did not give the commission to be enacted by human strength; God's power was also promised (v. 49). This promise is identical to the one recorded in Acts (1:3-8). The power promised by the Father is adequate to fulfill the task of witnessing, but the disciples were to remain in the city of Jerusalem until God's power came upon them.

4. *The Ascension, 24:50-53.* During the forty-day period following the resurrection (Acts 1:3-4) Jesus appeared numerous times to His disciples, teaching concerning the nature of the kingdom and their basic responsibilities relating to it. Jesus had finished the earthly ministry assigned by the Father; the work of atonement had been completed. The resurrected Christ was now prepared to ascend to the right hand of the Father. Jesus led the disciples to the Mount of Olives near Bethany, where He lifted his hands and blessed them. Perhaps this was reminiscent of the high priest, who upon retiring from the Temple on the feast days, lifted his hands and blessed the people. The Messiah, who had now completed the work of atonement, lifted His hands as a gesture to indicate divine blessing upon His disciples. While blessing His disciples, He was carried from them into heaven.

The grandeur of God's revelation and earthly manifestation in Jesus Christ overwhelmed those who observed the scene. They worshiped Him and returned to Jerusalem with indescribable joy. The disciples, remaining continually in the Temple, blessed God.

Luke gave numerous proofs of Jesus' resurrection, but likely in the minds of the disciples none surpassed that of the ascension. Returning with jubilant expressions of joy, the disciples were preparing to begin the task assigned by Jesus.

Luke opened his gospel with the scene in the Temple; he concludes the account in the same manner. He began with a question on the part of Zacharias; he concludes with a note of joy triumphantly ringing in the hearts of the disciples. Luke has prepared his reader for the activities described in the Acts of the Apostles.

FOR FURTHER STUDY

1. Read the articles entitled "Council" and "Sanhedrin" in *The Westminister Dictionary of the Bible*, pp. 117-118, 533.
2. Read the article entitled "Provinces" in *The Interpreter's Dictionary of the Bible*, pp. 940-941.

3. Read the article entitled "Pilate" in *The Zondervan Pictorial Bible Dictionary*, pp. 656-657. Characterize Pilate. Compare the synoptic references to him (Matthew 27:1-30; Mark 15:1-15; Luke 23:1-24). Does John (18:28-40) give additional information?

4. Read the article entitled "Cross" in *The New Smith's Bible Dictionary*, p. 75.

5. Employing a Bible concordance, list the many evidences of Jesus' resurrection.

6. Do Luke 24:50-53 and Acts 1:4-9 describe the same event? Read F. F. Bruce, "The Acts of the Apostles" in *The New International Commentary on the New Testament*, pp. 39-48.